What experts are saying about
Parenting Is Heart Work

"Wow! Parenting Is Heart Work is simply a masterpiece! It's got it all. This book has my highest recommendation. That's why we've chosen it to be our resource for parents at AWANA this year!"
—LARRY FOWLER, EXECUTIVE DIRECTOR, AWANA CLUBS INTERNATIONAL

"I have never seen a better book on reaching a child's heart. As parents we are too quick to correct and miss a chance to connect to the heart of a child."
—STEPHEN ARTERBURN, FOUNDER, NEW LIFE MINISTRIES

"Parenting Is Heart Work *resonated deep within me. This book clearly describes a biblically sound, practical approach to parenting, and I am happy to endorse it."*
—ARCHIBALD D. HART, PH.D., FPPR, SENIOR PROFESSOR OF PSYCHOLOGY AND DEAN EMERITUS, GRADUATE SCHOOL OF PSYCHOLOGY, FULLER THEOLOGICAL SEMINARY

"We are so excited about this book at AWANA that we want to get it into the hands of every parent whose children are in our children's programs."
—DR. GREG CARLSON, AWANA

"Scott Turansky and Joanne Miller have taken an essential element of parenting and given us practical ideas to put into practice."
—JOSH D. MCDOWELL, JOSH MCDOWELL MINISTRY

"Parenting Is Heart Work *is a positively brilliant resource for parents. This is a must read for any parent concerned about shaping the hearts of their children."*
—ROB GASKILL, CHRISTIANITY TODAY INTERNATIONAL

"This is a thoughtful, practical, and encouraging book."
—ROGER W. SCHMURR, SENIOR EDITOR, *CHRISTIAN HOME & SCHOOL* MAGAZINE

"This book will help parents learn how to shepherd their children into a deeper relationship with the Lord, His Word, and other people as they grow."
—DON MCCLURE, PASTOR, CALVARY CHAPEL, LAGUNA, CA

"Scott Turansky and Joanne Miller nail it. Straightforward and practical, Parenting Is Heart Work *is great.*"

—ERIC AND JENNIFER GARCIA,
FOUNDERS, ASSOCIATION OF MARRIAGE AND FAMILY MINISTRIES

PSYCHOLOGISTS AND COUNSELORS

"The authors skillfully combine expertise, personal experiences, and professional work to help parents understand their own hearts and the influence they have on their kids' hearts."

—KARL BENZIO, MD,
CHRISTIAN PSYCHIATRIST AND DIRECTOR OF LIGHTHOUSE NETWORK

"This book provides a superb manual for connecting with your children's emotions, impacting their thinking, and leading them to genuine heart change."

—GEORGE MAY, PASTOR OF COUNSELING, CALVARY CHURCH, LANCASTER, PA

"This book connected with my soul, bringing tears to my eyes. It takes you to a whole new level of parenting. I will use these ideas in my Family Ministry class."

—DR. JOHN McMURPHY, ASSOCIATE PROFESSOR OF CHILDREN'S MINISTRY,
CAROLINA EVANGELICAL DIVINITY SCHOOL

"This is a great addition to parents' arsenal on the sometimes perplexing challenges of raising children."

—JEFFREY S. BLACK, PH.D.,
CHAIR, GRADUATE DIVISION, DEPARTMENT OF CHRISTIAN COUNSELING,
PHILADELPHIA BIBLICAL UNIVERSITY

HOMESCHOOL LEADERS

"This excellent and very practical book is one I wholeheartedly recommend to every parent!"

—MARILYN HOWSHALL, AUTHOR OF *WISDOM'S WAY OF LEARNING*

"We will be using this book and recommending it at homeschool conferences and in the single mom's parenting class we're involved with."

—JEFF MYERS, MYERS INSTITUTE

"I am impressed with the clear distinction between behavioral modification and heart motivation. I recommend all parents read this book."

—BRUCE EAGLESON, MD,
ALLIANCE OF CHRISTIAN HOME EDUCATION LEADERSHIP

"Parenting Is Heart Work *is profound—it provides the connection!"*

—DIANA WARING,
INTERNATIONALLY KNOWN SPEAKER AND HOMESCHOOLING AUTHOR

PASTORS

"A generous supply of real-life examples shows how heart change is possible. I encourage parents, teachers, and pastors to read this book and implement it!"

—TOM GIVENS, PASTOR, GRACE BAPTIST CHURCH,
SANTA CLARITA, CA

"This is a book of encouragement and how-to's that will change your family dynamic."

—MIKE MACINTOSH,
PASTOR, HORIZON CHRISTIAN FELLOWSHIP, SAN DIEGO, CA

"As a Family Minister I found this book to be a wonderful resource that I will put in the hands of our parents."

—GAIL HATMAKER,
CHILDREN'S PASTOR, FIRST BAPTIST CHURCH, WINDERMERE, FL

"Practical. Practical. Practical! I would highly recommend this book for any parent who is challenged by the amazing complexity of raising a child in today's culture."

—LLOYD PULLEY, PASTOR, CALVARY CHAPEL, OLD BRIDGE, NJ

"This book provides a wonderful tool that is useful for not only understanding the human heart, but also for remedying the ills that spring forth from that same heart."

—DAVID ROSALES, PASTOR AND AUTHOR OF
RAISING RIGHT-HEARTED KIDS IN A WRONG-WAY WORLD

MINISTRY LEADERS

"Scott Turansky and Joanne Miller have again captured the essence of grace-filled parenting. Their research on the heart and its relationship to communication is simple, yet profound."

—JOHN ERWIN, PRESIDENT AND FOUNDER,
NATIONAL ASSOCIATION OF FAMILY MINISTRIES

"This book just became our number one recommendation for parents we work with around the world ... a must read for any season of family life."

—GORDON AND BECKI WEST, KIDZ AT HEART INTERNATIONAL

"By the end of the first chapter, I was hooked. Parenting Is Heart Work *is filled with useful examples and how-to strategies."*
—KIRK WEAVER, EXECUTIVE DIRECTOR, FAMILY TIME TRAINING

"Scott Turansky and Joanne Miller have done a masterful job of showing us the difference between modifying behavior and changing the heart."
—GARY SPRAGUE, PRESIDENT, CENTER FOR SINGLE-PARENT FAMILY MINISTRY

"Through our ministry we'll definitely be sharing this book with thousands of families who will benefit from its message, including mine!"
—MARK MERRILL, PRESIDENT, FAMILY FIRST

*"*Parenting Is Heart Work *is a practical combination of science, art, and biblical principles. We highly recommend it as must reading by every parent and grandparent."*
—BOB AND YVONNE TURNBULL, SPEAKERS, AUTHORS, AND LIFE COACHES

"I recommend, without reservation, this latest work from the biblical parenting experts Turansky and Miller."
—PAUL PETTIT, PRESIDENT AND FOUNDER, DYNAMIC DADS

"I found Parenting Is Heart Work *valuable with practical and compassionate teaching. It will yield surprising and delightful results."*
—DAN SCHMIDT, VICE PRESIDENT, BIBLE CLUB MOVEMENT INTERNATIONAL

"Scott Turansky and Joanne Miller have profound insight into the great frontier of parenting—understanding and motivating the heart."
—DR. MAC PIER, CONCERTS OF PRAYER GREATER NEW YORK

"I believe what you read in this book truly is God's answer to the crisis the families are facing today in raising children in this last generation."
—DR. K. P. YOHANNAN, FOUNDER AND PRESIDENT, GOSPEL FOR ASIA

"This book will transform your approach to parenting. Don't underestimate the value of parenting the heart."
—PASTOR KARL BASTIAN, CHILDREN'S PASTOR, FOUNDER, KIDOLOGY

"Scott Turansky and Joanne Miller have discovered the pulse of God and Parenting Is Heart Work *is beating right along with it!"*
—REV. KIM MOORE, THE CENTER ON CHRISTIAN RELATIONSHIPS

"GREAT book! This book shows parents how to guide children to a healthy, successful life, and presents a parenting method that is loving and nurturing."
—MOE AND PAIGE BECNEL, BLENDING A FAMILY MINISTRY

Parenting is *Heart* WORK

Dr. Scott Turansky
Joanne Miller, RN, BSN

David C Cook

transforming lives together

PARENTING IS HEART WORK
Published by David C. Cook
4050 Lee Vance View
Colorado Springs, CO 80918 U.S.A.

David C. Cook Distribution Canada
55 Woodslee Avenue, Paris, Ontario, Canada N3L 3E5

David C. Cook U.K., Kingsway Communications
Eastbourne, East Sussex BN23 6NT, England

David C. Cook and the graphic circle C logo
are registered trademarks of Cook Communications Ministries.

The names of people who have come to Effective Parenting for counseling
have been changed. Some illustrations combine individual stories in order to protect
confidentiality. Stories of the authors' children have been used by permission.

Effective Parenting is a nonprofit corporation committed to the communication of sound,
biblical parenting principles through teaching; counseling; and publishing written, audio,
and video materials. A video series, "Parenting Is Heart Work," is also available.
To obtain a complete resource list or have Dr. Scott Turansky and Joanne Miller
present their material live, you may contact:

Effective Parenting
76 Hopatcong Dr.
Lawrenceville, NJ 08648-4136
800-771-8334

www.EffectiveParenting.org
parent@effectiveparenting.org

Library of Congress Cataloging-in-Publication Data

Turansky, Scott, 1957-
Parenting is heart work / by Scott Turansky and Joanne Miller.
p. cm.
ISBN 978-0-7814-4152-0
1. Child rearing–Religious aspects–Christianity. I. Miller, Joanne, 1960- II. Title.
BV4529.T89 2006
248.8'45–dc22
2005022014

Cover Design: Two Moore Designs/Ray Moore
Cover Photo: ©istockphoto

Printed in the United States of America
First Edition 2006

10 11 12 13 14 15 16 17 18 19

100709

Contents

PART 4: TOUCHING YOUR CHILD'S HEART

How to Use This Book

A parent's job can get complicated at times. We want this book to be a catalyst for change in your family. You may find that just reading this book gives you the practical ideas you want now. Often exchanging ideas with your spouse or others sparks new approaches to parenting. You may discover more insight as you work through the concepts with other parents. You may even read parts of this book with your kids to stimulate discussions with them about becoming a heart-based family.

Keep in mind that the readers' guide at the end of this book contains questions for group discussion corresponding to every chapter. You may choose to combine the chapters and their questions to complete the book in a ten-week or thirteen-week study.

If you'd like further in-depth teaching with this book, you may want to use the eight-part video series by the same title. It contains a leader's guide and an eight-part children's program curriculum, so that children are learning things that complement what the adults are learning. You'll find more information about other resources at the back of this book.

We trust you'll enjoy this book as much as we have enjoyed writing it.

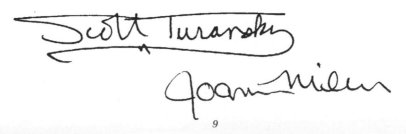

Introduction:
See with New Eyes

"The LORD does not look at the things man looks at. Man looks at the outward appearance, but the LORD looks at the heart."

1 SAMUEL 16:7

A Heart Story from the Bible

Samuel was discouraged. He'd worked so hard to help King Saul do the right thing. But even though Saul started well, it was becoming more and more clear he wasn't the best one for the job. *If he'd only change. He could be such a good king. The people need him. I wish he'd follow the Lord.*

The Lord interrupted Samuel's thoughts. "It's time to move on, Samuel. I've rejected Saul as king. I want you to anoint someone else. Get things ready for a trip."

Samuel recognized God speaking. After all, he'd been listening to the voice of the Lord ever since he was a child. So he obeyed the Lord and went to Bethlehem, where he met the family of Jesse. Samuel knew that it was from this family God would choose a new king. It would be his job to anoint God's chosen one. *I wonder which one of the boys God will choose to be the king?*

When Samuel saw Eliab, Jesse's oldest son, he knew he must be the one. He was tall and good-looking like Saul. He'd make a great leader for Israel. *He's the kind of person that people will follow.*

But wait. God interrupted his thoughts again. "Samuel, there's something you don't understand. There's something I have to teach you."

Samuel paused and looked around at the family gathering in front of him. He was there with them, but his thoughts were in a different place, listening to God.

"Do not consider his appearance or his height, for I have rejected him. The Lord does not look at the things man looks at. Man looks at the outward appearance but the Lord looks at the heart."

Yes, it makes sense! Why didn't I realize it before? Sure, God's measuring stick is different. He looks at the heart. Oh, if I only would have seen that earlier; maybe I could have better prepared Saul as king. Maybe I could have challenged him more on a heart level. Yes, this is God's way. It's so important. This will change the way I work with people. God is interested in the heart!

Samuel continued to follow God's lead and discovered that David, who was just a boy at the time, was God's choice for a new king. Samuel anointed him, celebrated with the family for a while, then started on his way. That day, Samuel not only learned who'd be the next king of Israel, but he learned a little more about how God works with people. Samuel learned that God is more interested in the heart than in outward appearance.

For the rest of Samuel's days, he, too, would think differently. He'd try to think about others the way God thinks about them. He wouldn't just look at their behavior. He'd consider their hearts.

(This story was taken from 1 Samuel 16:1–13.)

See with New Eyes

God wants to revolutionize our thinking about parenting. In the same way he challenged Samuel to adopt a completely different approach to identifying a king, God wants us to embrace a foundational principle for our families.

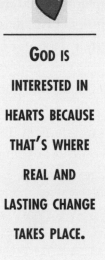

GOD IS INTERESTED IN HEARTS BECAUSE THAT'S WHERE REAL AND LASTING CHANGE TAKES PLACE.

God has a heart-based approach to working with people. This same truth changes many of the strategies and approaches parents use with their kids. God is interested in hearts because that's where real and lasting change takes place. In fact, when you direct your energies toward your child's heart, amazing things will happen.

Lou and Holly came to our office for family counseling. Their thirteen-year-old daughter, Kelly, did what they asked, but she usually had a bad attitude. She said she hated her parents because of the limits they placed on her. The walls in family dynamics were thick, and continual tension dominated their home. Lou and Holly wanted help.

We suggested trying a heart-based approach. Their blank stares revealed they had no idea what we were talking about, so we started at the beginning. Over several weeks, we trained these parents to think differently about parenting, but it wasn't easy. It seemed like every time we discussed a new dimension of family life or unpacked another problem, we discovered related problems that required a different way of thinking.

Lou and Holly had established habits of behavior modification with their daughter. "You can't go out until you clean your room." "We'll buy you some new clothes if you get better grades." Kelly expected a certain pattern from her parents, which made change all the more challenging. We offered a number of ideas and approaches to break the dangerous mold their daughter had grown accustomed to.

Over several weeks, Lou and Holly made significant inroads into their daughter's heart. Small steps of improvement grew into occasional deeper conversations. The parents saw changes in Kelly's behavior, but more important, they could feel things improving on a deeper level. Cooperation around the house increased, and they even began receiving good reports about her from school. It took some time, but these parents made a major parenting shift, and all their hard work paid off dramatically. In our final session, Mom shared a touching story:

> **TOUCHING OUR KIDS' HEARTS IS POSSIBLE, BUT IT TAKES SOME TIME AND PLANNING SO WE'RE READY FOR THE OPPORTUNITIES WHEN THEY COME.**

"I had to confront Kelly because she missed an assignment at school. In the past, she would have attacked me with anger and accusations, refusing to accept responsibility, but this time was different. She said, 'I know. I made a mistake and procrastinated. I'm not going to do that again. I'm sorry.'

"I was floored. I didn't know quite how to respond. She took me by surprise, so I said okay and walked out.

"Later she came to me and said, 'Mom, I just want you to know I really am going to try harder at school. Thanks for all you do for me.'

"I felt like crying as I hugged her. It was one of those 'touching heart' moments that I'll always treasure."

Touching our kids' hearts is possible, but it takes some time and planning so we're ready for the opportunities when they come. Of course, many current parenting trends don't even acknowledge the heart. They emphasize behavior modification. "If you get your homework done, you can watch a movie tonight." "If you kids keep fighting, you'll have to play alone." "If you clean your room, you can have a friend over."

BEHAVIOR MODIFICATION APPEALS TO CHILDREN'S RESIDENT SELFISHNESS.

This approach of "Do what I say and I'll let you have what you want" often misses the heart altogether. In fact, it has the opposite effect of what parents want. Behavior modification appeals to children's resident selfishness. It may work at times, but it has a limited capacity to make lasting changes. Behavior modification gets old quickly. Parents find they must continually up the ante and offer bigger and bigger incentives to maintain the desired behavior. A focus on getting the right actions down teaches children image management. The message our children hear is that behavior is what's important. Who cares about the heart?

It's time for a heart revolution in parenting. Behavior modification often works for the short term, but it does little to mold a child's heart for the future. It's like building a house of cards. No foundation and no depth mean the child's whole life could fall apart at any moment.

There's much at stake in raising children. When we take a heart approach to parenting, we partner with God in raising a future generation. Children learn to make changes on the inside, not just outwardly. Those changes last and become the basis for conviction and values that our children will carry with them for the rest of their lives. A conscience develops to help guide them in decisions that involve right and wrong.

If you haven't had much experience working with the heart, then you're about to start a fascinating journey. You're going to learn a different way of relating to your children. You'll discover opportunities to touch your kids on a deeper level.

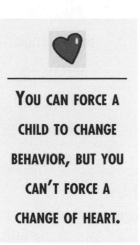

YOU CAN FORCE A CHILD TO CHANGE BEHAVIOR, BUT YOU CAN'T FORCE A CHANGE OF HEART.

Motivating heart change isn't easy. You can force a child to change behavior, but you can't force a change of heart. It's a deeper work. Helping children change their hearts requires a lot of thought, planning, and prayer. More and more parents are relearning discipline so that they can have a lasting impact on their children.

Please don't think that a heart-based approach to discipline is all mushy and lenient. It's not. Firmness and hard work produce character. The challenge is to help children change on a deeper level so they can become most effective in life.

So, where do you start? Let's look at the last two verses of the Old Testament, in which the prophet Malachi looks forward to what God will do in the last days. He wrote, "He will turn the hearts of the fathers to their children, and the hearts of the children to their fathers."

Real heart solutions in children's lives start with your own heart as a parent. As you consider ways to touch your child's heart, it's our prayer that God will do a deeper work in your own heart as well. Sometimes God uses children to reveal significant issues in Mom and Dad's lives. Don't hesitate to put the book down and allow God to do a deeper work in you. One truth we see over and over again is that parents have to change before their children will change.

We find that parents long to connect with their kids. You'd like to be close, but much of the work of family life wears on relationships. Getting the house cleaned up, finishing homework, making and cleaning up meals, and just keeping kids moving in the right direction all tax relationships. You want to connect on a deeper level, but it seems that much of life is working against you.

And the challenges seem to increase as kids get older. Teens need limits, but they're gone more, getting their social needs met outside of the home. Parenting battles become intense, and many parents spend the quiet moments resting up for the next challenge instead of looking for opportunities to connect on a heart level.

Some parents even lose the desire to be close to their children. Their kids have hurt, battered, and even abused them. These parents sometimes settle for the drudgery of getting through the day and have lost the vision for anything more significant. "You don't know my kids," they say.

After attending one of our weekend parenting seminars, one mom asked, "What you shared tonight was so practical and touching, but my kids are older. Is it too late?"

I could see the discouragement on her face. "How old are your children?"

"Seven and ten."

I smiled and assured her it wasn't too late. In fact, God changes people at all ages.

"But I thought the critical years were between birth and age five; by then a child's life is set."

Although it is true that children develop rapidly when they're young, and much of their character and personality takes shape at that age, the idea that children are hardened like concrete is a humanistic view of human growth. If you didn't believe in God, you'd be in rather sad shape when it comes to helping children change.

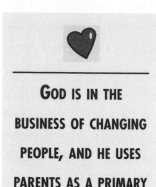

GOD IS IN THE BUSINESS OF CHANGING PEOPLE, AND HE USES PARENTS AS A PRIMARY TOOL TO FACILITATE THAT CHANGE IN CHILDREN'S LIVES.

The reality is that God does miracles in people's lives every day. God's Word molds adults' character regularly, and the Holy Spirit can change even the most stubborn or rebellious person into someone who emulates Christ. It's never too late. Don't let anyone, including your children, convince you otherwise. God is in the business of changing people, and he uses parents as a primary tool to facilitate that change in children's lives.

Consider this interesting picture from the Old Testament. When God designed the clothes that the high priest wore, he told the craftsmen to inscribe the names of the twelve tribes of Israel onto stones that they'd place on the breastplate so that "whenever Aaron enters the Holy Place, he will bear the names of the sons of Israel over his heart" (Ex. 28:29). There's a special application for parents in that verse.

We sometimes say children are a pain in the neck or they're getting in our hair. Try placing them over your heart. It's amazing what happens when you do. Kids notice the difference and respond accordingly. If you want your children to change their hearts, you must make praying for them a priority in your life.

Aaron entered the Holy Place to pray. The stones on the breastplate reminded him to pray for all those under his spiritual care. Pray for your children often. God not only works through prayer to change your kids, but he also uses your prayers to make you more sensitive to his work in their hearts. In your prayer time, be sure to listen as well as talk. God may clarify a direction or reveal something to you about your child that you haven't seen before. Aaron wore a breast-plate that contained a symbolic way to remember to keep the Israelites on his heart. You also probably have ways to do the same thing. If not, take some time and create them. You might consider a picture of your kids on the refrigerator or key chain, a Bible verse on your bathroom mirror, or a bracelet or other piece of jewelry that reminds you to keep your kids on your heart and pray for them often. Prayer is one of the ways God uses to turn the hearts of the parents to their children.

One mom tells this story: "I felt alone. My kids hated me. They were disrespectful and hurtful to each other and to me. My husband did little to help. He didn't know what to do, so he withdrew. I couldn't imagine continuing at this rate for the next ten years until my kids were out of the house; I had to do something.

"The heart idea intrigued me. It seemed like a good plan, but then again, I'd tried so many other good ideas that didn't seem to work. I knew I needed to make some changes in myself first. I prayed that God would change *my* heart, and he did! Then I began to look beyond behavior and see the hearts of my kids and what they needed on a deeper level. Step by step, I went to work, doing what I could to help my children change their hearts.

"At first, it seemed like an overwhelming task. But as I started to focus my energies, I saw change. I was encouraged to continue on, and great things started happening in our family. My husband saw that things were different and partnered with me in parenting. Together we continued to work.

"Life has dramatically changed in our home since last year. Instead of a battlefield every day, we now spend some enjoyable relationship times together in our family. I actually like being with my kids, and they're enjoying our family more than ever. We still have to correct and set limits, but by focusing on our kids' hearts, we avoid the battles of the past. I'm so glad we stopped our family from becoming more hurtful and painful. God turned us around in some beautiful ways."

Yes, this is possible in your family too, and it all starts with the heart. As you read this book, you'll prepare yourself to be a tour guide for one of the greatest adventures your family will ever experience. It's our prayer that God will reveal to you a new way of looking at people, just like he did with Samuel. This parenting approach is exciting—in part because you're working with God in the most sacred place on earth: the heart.

As you begin a heart approach with your kids, don't be surprised if God does some deeper work in you as well. After all, God isn't just concerned about your children. He's eager to develop your heart too. So, let him work in and through you and great things will happen. Always remember that your heart is special; it's where God lives and works.

Prayer

Lord, please help me to see my kids the way you see them. Sometimes I get so focused on their behavior problems that I just react. I want to help my children make lasting changes. I want to touch their hearts. Please show me what that means. And Lord, I invite you to point out areas in my heart that need your special touch. I look forward to living life in this new dimension with your leadership. Amen.

Part 1

Understanding the Heart

"Love the L*ORD your God with all your heart and with all your soul and with all your strength."*

DEUTERONOMY 6:5

A Heart Story
from the Bible

David had a dream in his heart. He wanted to build God a house. This was no ordinary house. It would be a magnificent work. *Yes, I will do it. I will build a temple for God. It will be my most important accomplishment.*

David had already set the stage. He had conquered Jerusalem and had taken it from the Jebusites. *Jerusalem should be the place where I build the temple.* He had fortified Jerusalem, and it became known as the City of David. Next, he had set up a tent and brought the ark of the covenant to Jerusalem. *Yes, the next step is to build God a house. I can hardly wait.*

The Bible tells us David "set his heart" on building the temple. It was his passion—his dream. *I'm going to build God a beautiful house—nothing but the best in every way. Cedar from Lebanon. Gold, bronze, and silver will add the finishing touches. It will be the most magnificent building ever.*

One morning the prophet Nathan came to visit David with news. "David, the Lord told me last night that you are not the one to build the house for him."

"What? But ... but ... I've got such a great idea for building his house."

"God says he's had just a tent up to now, and it's moved from here to there for hundreds of years. He never asked for a house from anyone."

"I know, but I love the Lord so much and I feel bad living in my beautiful palace, when God has just a tent. I have all these ideas...."

"David, the house for God is a good idea, but you're just not the one to do it. Here's what God wants you to know. These are his words to you: 'You and I have had a special relationship. I've guided you over the years, and you are a man after my own heart. But my work with you included wars and bloodshed, so I don't want you to be the one to build my house. After you die, I'm going to have your son Solomon build the temple. He's the one I've chosen for this job.'"

"Wow! My son. Well, I'm glad the temple will be built. But it was just so important to me. It was one of my life goals."

As Nathan left, David started thinking. *I have so many things to explain to Solomon. He has to do it right. He's young and inexperienced. Will he pick the right people? I've got to help him.*

When David set his heart on something, he was determined. He couldn't just walk away. *If I can't build it, then I will prepare everything for it.* He bought the land for the site from Araunah, who offered to give it to him free. But David said, "No, I'll pay full price. I can't offer sacrifices to the Lord from that which costs me nothing."

Because David's heart was committed, he was driven by his passion. He made extensive preparations for building the temple. He talked to workmen and managers. He ordered resources from all over the world. *I want this house to stand out—not just here in Israel but around the world.* David chose the stonecutters who would make the huge stones for the walls. He provided iron to make the hinges for the doors and gathered so much bronze that no one could even weigh it.

David also imported so many cedar logs from Lebanon that no one could count them, either. He collected 3,750 tons of gold and 37,500 tons of silver.

While other men's hobbies were hunting, horses, or collecting enemy artifacts, David's only hobby was making sure everything was ready for Solomon to build God's house. He made architectural drawings for the porches, the buildings, the storerooms, the upper parts, the inner rooms, and the place of atonement. It was all there. David didn't miss a detail. He made diagrams for all the equipment and utensils that would go into the temple. The plans told the weight of the metal in each cup, plate, and candlestick. David prescribed how much gold to put on each piece of furniture.

Solomon watched his dad work. He could see the passion in his father. Day after day, his dad told him about the plans to build the Lord's temple. "Son, I had it in my heart to build the temple, but God wants you to build it instead. God says you will be a man of peace and rest. Our country sure needs that after all the fighting I've had to do. But, son, please don't think you can take this job lightly. It's so important. This is God's house. Please put your heart into it as I've done."

Then David called all the leaders of Israel together. "Officials of Israel, I've had it in my heart to build a house for God, but he wants my son to build it instead. I am now charging all of you before your fellow countrymen and before God to help Solomon. Do what he tells you to do.

"And Solomon, here are all the plans you will need to build this house for God. I hope I've thought of everything. Be strong and courageous, son, and do the work. You have all the raw materials you need and you have all the people you need. Son, all you need now is the heart. Will you please set your heart on building this house?"

That's all David could do. He had to let it go and let God

do the rest through his son. David died soon after, but he'd have been pleased. Solomon rose to the task. He built a magnificent temple. It took seven years, but it had all the beauty David had imagined. David's passion endured long after his death, and the goal he set was accomplished. Although he didn't see it happen, he got what his heart desired. Through his son, he built the house for God.

(This story is taken from 2 Samuel 7, 1 Chronicles 22 and 28, and 1 Kings 6–8.)

Chapter 1

What Is the Heart?
(Part 1)

More than 750 verses in the Bible use the term *heart*. It's where longings grow, secrets are kept, pain is felt, plans are devised, commitments solidify, and character is developed. In short, the heart is a person's center, the deepest spot in one's life.

When you talk to yourself, you're doing work in your heart, sorting out issues, synchronizing them with other priorities and values, and preparing responses. Discouragement is felt in the heart, as well as anxiety, fear, and anger. Peace, joy, and love also produce their fruits in the heart.

Instead of working on the heart, many parents settle for simply changing their children's behavior. After all, you can see behavior and, most of the time, you can control it. The heart is a mysterious place over which you have little control. The work of understanding it, though, pays off well as you help your children make lasting changes. You experience greater closeness, and children develop maturity.

Before we can help you change your child's heart, you must first understand a little more about what it is, how it works, and what makes it tick. We want to help you understand how the Bible uses the word *heart* and then apply that understanding to your relationship with your children. Hold on; there's a lot here. Don't get bogged down—just let yourself experience an overview of what God's Word teaches about the heart.

The Bible talks about nine different functions of the heart. We'll discuss five in this chapter and four in the next. You'll find this reading stimulating as you develop new ways to work on your child's deeper issues.

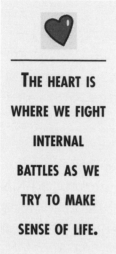

THE HEART IS WHERE WE FIGHT INTERNAL BATTLES AS WE TRY TO MAKE SENSE OF LIFE.

1. The Heart Is a Wrestling Place

First and foremost, the heart is where we fight internal battles as we try to make sense of life.

For example, Jesus knew the teachers of the law were struggling inside with the fact that he forgave the paralytic. In Matthew 9:4 he said, "Why do you entertain evil thoughts in your hearts?" Mary was intrigued by all the events of Jesus' birth, and the Bible says in Luke 2:19 that she pondered all these things in her heart. When the two disciples on the road to Emmaus realized their surprise guest was Jesus, they reflected on the experience by saying, "Were not our hearts burning within us while he talked with us on the road and opened the Scriptures to us?" (Luke 24:32).

When experience, teaching, and values need to be integrated into our lives, it happens in the workshop of our hearts. Information comes into our heads constantly, but much of it just stays there. Only what moves into our hearts becomes part of our lives.

When eight-year-old Jordan tells himself, "I'm no good. No one wants to be with me. I'll never get it right," he's filling his heart with negative images of himself. Rebecca feels good in her heart because she refused to join those who were disrespectful to their teacher. Jack's mom can see a heart problem because he scowls and complains whenever she asks him to do something. In their hearts, children wrestle with and come to conclusions about life and its challenges.

This deeper part of a person's life is often a mystery, leaving parents confused about how to effect any significant change in their children. Recognizing that the heart is a wrestling place gives parents the motivation to relate to their children on a deeper level.

2. The Heart Is the Place of Commitments and Determination

After the wrestling, children reach conclusions that turn into decisions and commitments. Jesus told the expert in the law that the greatest commandment is to "Love the Lord your God with all your heart" (Matt. 22:37). Paul encouraged the believers in Antioch to "remain true to the Lord with all their hearts" (Acts 11:23). Moses told the people, "Take to heart all the words I have solemnly declared to you this day.... They are your life" (Deut. 32:46–47). Proverbs 3:5 says, "Trust in the LORD with all your heart." Each of these verses is a call to commitment.

Commitments provide purpose, meaning, and direction. Without these, the heart lives in continual turmoil, tossed around by fear,

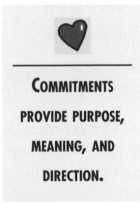

COMMITMENTS PROVIDE PURPOSE, MEANING, AND DIRECTION.

anger, or anxiety. Often, a continual problem with negative emotions indicates the need for some major heart work. Children need to understand more about life and how to process it and even adopt new teaching into their value systems.

Five-year-old Jerry decided he was going to help in Sunday school. Each Sunday when he got to church, he marched right in and looked for ways to help the teacher. Dad could see he had a commitment to help, and it affected the boy's whole Sunday experience. Dad looked for ways to encourage Jerry's heart commitment. Ralph, age fourteen, was determined to save money for a remote-controlled car. Mom told us, "He set his heart on getting that car and spent hours earning the money." Martha was committed to her friends but not to her schoolwork, requiring some major heart shifts to get her commitments into proper balance.

> AS PARENTS, WE LONG TO CONNECT WITH OUR CHILDREN IN MEANINGFUL WAYS.

Sometimes parents are encouraged by the commitments they see their children make, and other times red flags go up, warning parents to take action. Kids can become so focused on what they want that they get angry when they can't get it. Helping our children adjust and balance their commitments is part of the heartwork necessary to develop maturity in their lives.

3. The Heart Is Where We Feel Close to Others

In Acts 4:32, the early disciples "were one in heart and mind," a statement of their unity. Jonathan's armor-bearer expressed unity with his boss by saying, "Do all that you have in mind.... I am with you heart and soul" (1 Sam. 14:7).

In the end times, God will restore closeness in family life. Malachi 4:6 says, "He will turn the hearts of the fathers to their children, and the hearts of the children to their fathers."

On the other hand, people also can feel distant from others in their hearts. Michal, David's wife, didn't like how he was worshipping the Lord and "despised him in her heart" (2 Sam. 6:16).

As parents, we long to connect with our children in meaningful ways. When children are young, those special moments happen regularly, even daily. You read a book to your four-year-old every night, he leans on your arm, and you cherish those times of closeness. He's ready to believe everything you say. You play a card-matching game on the floor with your five-year-old, and she laughs and says, "You're fun to play with, Mommy." You correct your six-year-old, and he cries that repentant cry and wants a hug—and tears come to your eyes too, because you know you've connected with his heart.

These special moments of heart connection also happen with older children, but, in many families, they come less often. A fourteen-year-old gets a positive school report, giving her dad an opportunity to affirm her hard work. Her smile confirms he made the heart connection he'd hoped for. A seventeen-year-old gets fired from his job and wants to talk about it. His mom listens for a while and can tell her son appreciates her acceptance. You take your teenage son and his friends to the beach and try extra hard to relate in ways that don't embarrass your son. At the end of the day, one of the kids says, "Your mom is cool," and your son gives you that look of approval. You know you connected at heart level. The closeness you and your children feel (or don't feel) is a heart function.

4. The Heart Is Where We Experience Emotions

People usually recognize that the heart and emotions go together. In fact, some people see this aspect of the heart as the only one. They don't realize how many other parts of the heart affect a child. Many families ignore emotions or view them as a nuisance. Emotions affect children more than they realize, and it's important to put them in proper perspective and plan to deal with them in family life.

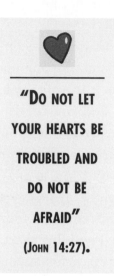

"DO NOT LET YOUR HEARTS BE TROUBLED AND DO NOT BE AFRAID"

(JOHN 14:27).

Jesus told his disciples, "Do not let your hearts be troubled and do not be afraid" (John 14:27). In Colossians 3:15, Paul wrote, "Let the peace of Christ rule in your hearts." The Mosaic law says, "Do not hate your brother in your heart" (Lev. 19:17). The king saw Nehemiah was troubled and said, "This can be nothing but sadness of heart" (Neh. 2:2). Proverbs 17:22 says, "A cheerful heart is good medicine."

Kyra, age six, struggled with fear. She was timid around others, hesitant to try new things, and afraid to go upstairs by herself. Mom had tried to coax her, sometimes gently and other times firmly, with little success. We began working with Kyra's heart. She had developed certain heart responses to life's challenges, believing she'd fail or get hurt in most circumstances. Together with her mom and dad, we explored her fears, taught her about trust and confidence, and then practiced some risk-taking activities. We taught her how to pray through her fears, and she memorized several Bible verses about trusting God and accomplishing things with his strength. Mom enrolled Kyra in a community soccer league, encouraged her to pay for something at the store, and sent her on "missions" to stretch her courage.

At the same time, Mom and Dad were careful to avoid pushing their daughter too far, condemning, or communicating undue frustration with what they perceived to be slow progress. After several months, improvement was obvious. Kyra was changing on a heart level, causing outward adjustments as well.

Joel's dog, Skippy, died. Joel, age thirteen, had raised that dog from a puppy. They had played together, slept together, and Joel had taken care of him when he was sick. Now his beloved friend was gone. His heart was broken; the pain was intense. He spent the next few days bouncing between lashing out at those around him and sitting quietly and introspectively. His heart was working hard to absorb this unwanted new experience: life without his friend.

Mom was patient with Joel, giving him space to grieve and work things out. She initiated conversation with him often and looked for ways to comfort him. Sometimes Joel used his sadness as an excuse for being unkind or disrespectful, but Mom made it clear that grieving was okay and meanness was not. Over time, Joel adjusted to life without Skippy. Mom's approach was successful because she considered Joel's heart during that time.

5. The Heart Is Where Temptations and Desires Develop

With commitments, determinations, and emotions all converging in the heart, it's no wonder temptation germinates there.

Matthew 6:21 says, "Where your treasure is, there your heart will be also." Psalm 37:4 says, "Delight yourself in the LORD and he will give you the desires of your heart." Solomon's "wives turned his heart after other gods" (1 Kings 11:4). Paul wrote, "My heart's desire and prayer to God for the Israelites is that they may be saved" (Rom. 10:1).

Clearly, desires aren't always bad; in fact, many human longings are good. Knowing the difference, however, can be a challenge at times. Of course, we all wish our children would desire the right things and avoid tempting situations. One mom saw her eight-year-old daughter was easily swayed by her friends. She looked for ways to help her daughter take a stand for righteousness. She talked with her daughter about what was right and wrong in various situations and helped her see what temptation is and how she was making some dangerous choices by giving in to her friends. The girl responded well to her mother and began to look for ways to stand for what's right.

A twelve-year-old asked his mom why she doesn't get angry when she gets cut off on the road, giving Mom a perfect opportunity to talk about how she lets it go so she doesn't have to harbor the anger. She knew he needed that message, because he'd been treated unfairly at school and was tempted to act out his own anger. He listened and pondered what she said. Mom watched the wheels turn in his head and knew she had just connected somewhere deep inside her son.

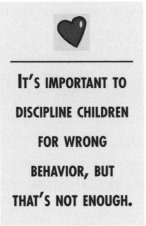

It's important to discipline children for wrong behavior, but that's not enough.

You've read about just five functions of the heart, but we hope you're already seeing yourself and your child on these pages. To command a child to "stop having a bad attitude" may draw attention to the child's problem, but it doesn't usually address the heart issues the attitude represents. Excusing a child's disrespect by saying, "At least he does what I tell him to do," focuses on behavior and misses an opportunity to do some deeper work.

It's important to discipline children for wrong behavior,

but that's not enough. Children often need help processing much of what they're wrestling with on the inside. Their feelings may dominate their decisions. They may long for closeness but not know how to get it. God has placed parents in a position in their children's lives to help this process.

Sometimes a well-meaning Christian will say something like, "I don't think it's possible to work on the heart. That's God's job. Children who haven't yet committed their lives to Christ can't change their hearts, so asking parents to do so is just a waste of time." Although it's true that supreme heart change takes place through the gift of salvation, God has given parents the responsibility to till the soil and teach their children how to respond to God's continual work

PARENTS ARE IN A GOD-GIVEN ROLE OF TEACHING THEIR CHILDREN EVERY DAY WHAT IT MEANS TO RESPOND TO GOD.

of grace in their lives. The Bible uses the term *repentance* to describe the personal responsibility we all have to change our hearts. God expects people to respond to him, and he calls them to repentance regularly in his Word. Parents are in a God-given role of teaching their children every day what it means to respond to God. When you understand your potential as a dad or mom in your child's life, you can understand the huge spiritual opportunity and responsibility God has given you.

The more you focus on your child's heart and consider a heart-based approach to child-training, the more ideas and solutions you'll discover. You might even want to take time to read each of the passages mentioned in this chapter and imagine yourself in the particular situation. See how God

addresses the hearts of those he works with and how significant change takes place.

Both from personal experience and from thousands of
families we've worked with, we find that parents must change
first before their children will change. How you work with
your children makes all the difference between progress and
hitting a brick wall. We've watched parents make significant
adjustments in the ways they parent—with amazing results.
As you consider the heart's functions, try to look at specific
ways you're presently working with your children. We'll give
you several more pointers in the chapters ahead.

Prayer

*Thank you for the things I can learn from my
children. Sometimes, Lord, my heart issues get in the
way of my parenting. Please give me insight into my
own life and make me a clean vessel for your use. I
look forward to what you're going to do in my children's lives. Please give me hope through even small
glimpses into their hearts. Amen.*

Chapter 2

What Is the Heart?
(Part 2)

God created the heart to be a person's central processing unit. When working correctly, the heart enables
children to mature and respond to life in productive ways.

Notice how the next four heart functions contribute to a
child's independence. Parents often wish their children would
have the maturity to deal with life with less parental involve-
ment. If the heart is in the right place, God uses it as a guide
to keep a person on track and moving in the right direction.

6. The Heart Experiences Guilt and Conviction of Sin

When Peter preached on Pentecost, people "were cut to the
heart" (Acts 2:37). When David cut off part of Saul's robe in
the cave, 1 Samuel 24:5 (KJV) says his "heart smote him."
David experienced conviction again when he counted the
fighting men (2 Sam. 24:10). In Psalm 51, after he sinned with
Bathsheba, David prayed to God, "Create in me a pure heart"
(v. 10) and cried, "The sacrifices of God are a broken spirit; a
broken and contrite heart" (v. 17).

The Holy Spirit convicts the hearts of people. Guilt's purpose is to point out sin in our lives and motivate us to deal

GUILT AFFECTS KIDS' HEARTS AND ROBS THEM OF PEACE.

with it. Sometimes you can just look at a child and see that he's guilty. He knows it. He can feel it. Guilt affects kids' hearts and robs them of peace.

A good correction routine gives children a chance to gain a clean slate by admitting wrong and asking forgiveness. Often, those steps do the necessary work of cleaning up the heart. After all, God says in 1 John 1:9, "If we confess our sins, he is faithful and just and will forgive us our sins and purify us from all unrighteousness."

Six-year-old Peter told his mom, "I have to tell you something. Last week I broke the glass ornament off your dresser; then I hid it in my room. Here it is. I'm sorry." Peter's mom valued the ornament but loved her son even more. "Your heart was bothering you all week, wasn't it? You did the right thing by coming and telling me about it. I'll miss my ornament, but your heart is more important than anything like this. I'm glad you decided to make it right. Come here and give me a hug. I forgive you."

Guilt is experienced in the heart, motivating children to cover up wrongdoing, blame others, or justify it—or confess and make things right. As you help your children process their offenses, you can do some significant heart work. A clear and strong conscience becomes a valuable ally as children maneuver through life's challenges.

7. The Heart Experiences Passion

Hezekiah was a good king who served the Lord with all his heart (2 Chron. 31:21). The book of Psalms says, "I will praise you, O LORD, with all my heart" (9:1) and "I seek you with all my heart" (119:10). In each of these verses, the word *heart* communicates the idea of passion.

When people do something wholeheartedly, they're doing it with zest and determination. Sometimes we say he put his heart into a job, or she has a heart for what she's doing.

Juan loved to play with his new video game. Every spare moment, he tried to get to the next level and improve his skills and techniques. Mom felt Juan was overdoing it a bit, so she established video-game time limits and looked for more constructive outlets for Juan's passion in life. Because Juan is a determined and passionate person, she knew part of her job was to continually direct him into more appropriate activities.

> **PART OF GROWING UP IS KNOWING WHEN TO INVEST EMOTIONALLY IN SOMETHING, WHAT TO GET PASSIONATE ABOUT.**

Some children have a tendency toward intensity in their lives. They seem to do everything with passion. This may be okay when they're achieving their goals, but when other people get in their way and they react with unkindness, their passion creates a problem. Part of growing up is knowing when to invest emotionally in something, what to get passionate about. When you help children in this area, you're contributing to an important aspect of their hearts.

8. The Heart Chooses Values to Hold and Convictions to Live By

All parents long for their children to establish convictions that will carry them through tough times. Sometimes those convictions help them control their own emotions. Other times,

RESPONSIBILITY, IN PART, IS STAYING TRUE TO PERSONAL VALUES EVEN WHEN NO ONE IS WATCHING.

that internal foundation helps them do what's right when others are tempting them to do wrong. Responsibility, in part, is staying true to personal values even when no one is watching. It's been said you can tell a lot about who a person really is by what he does in private, not just how he acts in front of others. Convictions become the moral pillars in our lives that keep us on track.

Moses told the people to put the commands of God "upon your hearts" (Deut. 6:6). When David described the righteous person in Psalm 37:31, he wrote, "The law of his God is in his heart; his feet do not slip." "Daniel purposed in his heart that he would not defile himself with the portion of the king's meat" (Dan. 1:8 KJV). When Jeremiah described the new covenant God would establish, he wrote that it would be different from the stone tablets of the old covenant. God said, "I will put my law in their minds and write it on their hearts" (Jer. 31:33).

Jack decided he wouldn't watch a certain TV show at his friend's house because he knew his parents wouldn't approve. Marlene believed that killing animals was wrong, so she told her mom she wanted to become a vegetarian. Marvin chose to turn in the watch he found at school because he knew keeping it would be wrong. These kids wanted to hold true to something they believed in. Those convictions determined the choices they made.

Some children do a better job of developing convictions than others, but all need guidance in this area. When should you stand up for yourself and when should you be a servant?

What does honesty look like in tough situations? How do you balance telling the truth and being gracious?

Your children likely have convictions already. Do you know what they are? What convictions are you trying to pass on? Do you have a plan for teaching them? These are heart issues and become the schoolhouse for the family.

9. The Heart Is Where We Connect with God

Romans 10:9–10 says a key to salvation is when you "believe in your heart that God raised him from the dead." Paul asked God to strengthen the Ephesians with power "so that Christ may dwell in your hearts" (Eph. 3:17). Paul wrote in 2 Corinthians 1:22 that God has put his Spirit "in our hearts as a deposit, guaranteeing what is to come." In Jeremiah 24:7, the prophet wrote that God will give the people a heart to know him, that he is the Lord. Jesus said, "These people honor me with their lips, but their hearts are far from me" (Matt. 15:8) about people who didn't know God personally.

IT'S IN THE HEART WHERE WE GET TO KNOW GOD IN A PERSONAL WAY.

It's in the heart where we get to know God in a personal way. He's chosen to live in our hearts—the central place in our lives—and when he does, he sets things in order. He organizes our priorities, rearranges our values, and reveals sin that must be addressed. Parents often become the hands and feet God uses to mold a child's heart. Our job is to find out where God is working and then partner with him to do the deeper work necessary in our kids' lives.

This Is a Little Deep for Me

Proverbs 20:5 says, "The purposes of a man's heart are deep waters." The implication is that the heart is a hard place to get to at times, complicated to understand, and difficult to adjust.

Extra time and energy are required to make heart connections with our kids. Some parents find this approach daunting. "What do I do about my day-to-day problems? How do I handle the misbehavior I see now? Changing the heart sounds great, but I have to make sure he gets his homework done tonight."

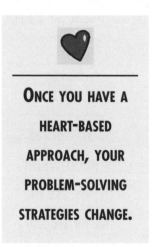

ONCE YOU HAVE A HEART-BASED APPROACH, YOUR PROBLEM-SOLVING STRATEGIES CHANGE.

It's true that sometimes we just have to get through the day. But once you have a heart-based approach, your problem-solving strategies change. With your new outlook, even day-to-day discipline has a long-range view. Sure, it takes time, but the alternative is scary. Focusing only on behavior often allows children to develop deep heart problems that eventually manifest themselves in tragic ways.

Many parents are lured into believing that if the to-do list items are checked off, it was a successful day. Unfortunately, if the heart issues aren't addressed, then eventually they create bigger problems than you ever imagined. Teenage rebellion doesn't start at age thirteen; it starts much earlier, in a young child's heart. Sometimes parents are shocked when their teenagers get involved with drugs or sex or get in trouble with the law. But heart issues rarely appear suddenly; they grow over time. Parents who discipline from a heart perspective learn to see and address deeper issues before they turn into bigger problems.

The Biggest Asset for Heart Change

God is in the business of changing hearts. Religion often focuses on behavior—doing certain things that might please God. But the Bible teaches something very different: Salvation is a relationship with God that does a deep work, changing the configuration of one's heart. As a result, our desires change and our will determines to do different things. Naturally, the resulting behavior falls in line with what God is doing in the heart. In this way, people are transformed from the inside out.

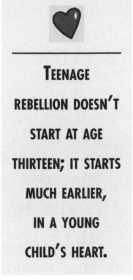

TEENAGE REBELLION DOESN'T START AT AGE THIRTEEN; IT STARTS MUCH EARLIER, IN A YOUNG CHILD'S HEART.

The best decision your child can make is to allow God to do the consecrating work of salvation in his or her life. We often use the words "Ask Jesus to come into your heart" because they describe how deeply people's lives change when they become Christians. Their longings and desires change. Their strategies and plans focus on a different goal. Peace replaces guilt, anger, and fear.

But even the most consecrated person struggles with sin. It's a heart issue. Some children just naturally have open hearts, and they learn quickly, repent often, and change on a deeper level. Then there are the other 99 percent of children who need parental initiative to help create those teachable moments and build the inner fortitude needed to follow the Lord in every area of their lives.

A spiritual battle is raging for our children's hearts. In today's world, parents can't be complacent and just hope everything will turn out okay. When Jesus prayed in the

Garden of Gethsemane, he did serious business with the Father, praying intensely for the upcoming challenges. Jesus asked Peter, James, and John to pray also, but they fell asleep instead. They had no idea of the spiritual challenge Jesus was facing and the danger they were all in as a result. When Jesus took a break from praying and found them sleeping, he said, "Watch and pray." Unfortunately,

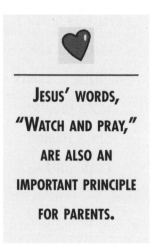

JESUS' WORDS, "WATCH AND PRAY," ARE ALSO AN IMPORTANT PRINCIPLE FOR PARENTS.

they went back to sleep, unaware of the increasing danger. A short time later, the guards came into the garden to arrest Jesus. Peter jumped up and started swinging a sword, contributing to the problem and creating another mess for Jesus to clean up.

Today, some parents are like Peter. They aren't ready for the challenges of parenting, and they just start swinging swords or attacking kids instead of working with the Lord to solve the problems.

Over and over again, as you read this book, you'll see that spiritual nourishment is a major source of heart development. Don't run over those paragraphs too quickly. Do you have spiritual resources to share with your children? God wants to give them to you.

In fact, the greatest parenting tip we could share with you is this: Maintain a strong connection to your heavenly Father. He offers spiritual guidance and direction to help you work through your own heart issues so you can be more effective with your children.

Jesus' words, "Watch and pray," are also an important principle for parents. Start watching your child's heart.

Become more aware of the deeper problems. Ask God to show you the real issues your son or daughter is facing. Then pray. Spend time talking to the Lord about your child's heart issues. Becoming more aware and seeking God's guidance are the first steps to successfully addressing the heart.

Now that you've explored what the heart is, you may feel a bit overwhelmed. In the coming chapters, we'll help you make more sense of these rather complex concepts. But first, we wanted you to get a glimpse of the depth of the heart. When you see how many facets it has, we pray you'll be motivated to see beyond your children's behavior and into their hearts.

Prayer

Lord, I pray the same prayer David prayed in Psalm 139:23: "Search me, O God, and know my heart; test me and know my anxious thoughts." Please point out areas in my heart that are getting in the way of my effectiveness with my family. I want to serve you here at home, and I ask you to prepare me every day for the difficult work of parenting. I also ask you to make me sensitive to my children's heart needs. Help me to see past the mundane tasks of the day to the deeper issues in their lives. Please use me as an instrument in the work you're doing in their hearts. Amen.

Chapter 3

Will I or Won't I?

The heart is the deepest part of one's life. Once issues are addressed on this foundational level, we move to another platform: the will. The heart makes commitments; the will makes choices based on those commitments.

In Exodus 35, God had given instructions about building a tabernacle, and the people were to donate the materials needed for the job. Verse 29 (KJV) says, "The children of Israel brought a willing offering unto the LORD, every man and woman, whose heart made them willing to bring for all manner of work, which the LORD had commanded to be made by the hand of Moses." Notice in that verse how the heart affects the will.

In Deuteronomy 30, when Moses spoke to the people about their commitment to the Lord, he used the word *heart* eight times. Then, in verse 19, he called them to make a choice: "I have set before you life and death, blessings and curses. Now choose life, so that you and your children may live." Once a commitment is made in the heart, the will chooses to do the right thing.

The will is that place of determination. The level of one's determination is affected by such things as personality,

A WISE PARENT HELPS TURN POTENTIAL FIGHTS AROUND, LOOKS FOR WAYS TO REDIRECT A CHILD'S INTENSITY, AND KNOWS WHEN TAKING A STAND AGAINST A CHILD'S WILL IS THE MOST LOVING THING TO DO.

character, values, and one's sense of morality. Parents and children often experience conflict when their wills determine to go in opposite directions. A wise parent helps turn potential fights around, looks for ways to redirect a child's intensity, and knows when taking a stand against a child's will is the most loving thing to do.

Strong-Willed Kids

Children who make decisions with intensity tend to be called "strong willed." At the end of the day, their parents feel as if they've been engaged in hand-to-hand combat for hours—and the children often win! All children fall somewhere on the continuum between strong willed and unmotivated, depending on their intensity level about life. Strong-willed kids are generally determined, highly motivated, persistent, and not easily persuaded once they've made up their minds. Most parents consider a strong will a negative personality trait because it often creates resistance and frustration in family life.

Four-year-old Michael wouldn't stay in bed. Mom had to send him back to bed several times each night. She said to us, "This is torture. Even if I yell and get angry, it doesn't seem to faze him. Nothing I do works. It's not fair. I work with him all day. I ought to get a little relief in the evening before I go to bed myself."

Michael's mom is right that her son should go to bed and

not keep getting up. We gave her a plan to deal with her son's determination. By sitting in her son's doorway and immediately responding when he started to get out of bed, she saw some improvement. We encouraged her to remain calm but firmly put him back to bed.

The next week, she said, "The first few nights, I must have put him back into bed twenty times, but after that things started to improve. In fact, now I can stay there for just a few seconds and then leave him." Three weeks later, she reported, "It's going well. I keep checking, and he stays in bed. It's like he needed me to show him I meant business. Now I can relax in the evenings, knowing Michael won't get up."

A STRONG WILL KEEPS A CHILD MOVING IN A CERTAIN DIRECTION IN SPITE OF OBSTACLES.

A strong will keeps a child moving in a certain direction in spite of obstacles. Often these children need bigger barriers or tighter limits to teach them that those boundaries are firm. On the other hand, the strong-willed child accomplishes things in life, because the roadblocks that might hold others back are no match for this kid's determination.

Joe, age eleven, found an injured cat in the neighborhood. He felt sorry for the cat and was determined to help it get well. He put the cat in a box, carried it home, and pleaded with Mom to take it to the vet. He fed the animal with an eye dropper and watched it intently for days. Eventually the cat did get well—but only because Joe didn't give up.

Joe's strong will was fed by his heart. He had compassion, valued life, and took on the challenge. His intensity paid off;

but even if the cat had died, Joe was doing what he believed was right.

Miriam's ten-year-old son, Alex, is strongly determined to do well at school. When he gets an assignment due in two weeks, he starts on it right away. Mom is pleased that Alex is diligent in school and praises him for his determination. His strong will comes from a sense of responsibility to do his work. (Of course, Mom wishes her other two children had that same strength.) It's a gift, and Alex will do well in life if he keeps it up.

CHILDREN WITH STRONG WILLS HAVE THE POTENTIAL TO BECOME THE NEXT GENERATION OF LEADERS.

Children with strong wills have the potential to become the next generation of leaders. They have their own ideas and plans. They know what they want. They're persistent, confident, passionate, and determined to succeed at whatever they choose to do. Leaders have an agenda, look for ways to incorporate others into their plans, and have a higher need for control in life. Balanced with graciousness, leaders become a treasure because they make things happen, create organization out of chaos, and motivate people to action.

Unfortunately, it's hard to raise a leader. These kids always have their own ways of doing things and like to tell other people (including their parents) what to do. Many parents of strong-willed children wish their kids were more compliant. Yet, in reality, it's the strong-willed kids who are often better equipped to succeed, be creative, and face adversity.

Of course, a strong-willed child can also be defiant and

rebellious. Many prisons are full of strong-willed people. The key, of course, is something deeper than the will. It's the heart. When the heart is in the right place, it guides the will in the right direction.

The Unmotivated Child

Unmotivated children are generally passive, cooperative, flexible, easygoing, and accommodating. These children may be easier to get along with because they lack the drive of strong-willed people. Still, even unmotivated children can be strong willed sometimes; it's just not their general tendency.

Marcus is content to let others lead. When his friend George comes over to play, Marcus lets him pick the game and decide when they'll move on to something else. George tells Marcus what to do, and Marcus seems content to follow along. Mom, who's rather strong willed herself, feels uncomfortable with the situation. She wishes Marcus would be the leader. Marcus needs to learn to lead at times, especially if George wants to do something that is wrong, but Mom needs to let Marcus be Marcus. She may need to adjust her expectations, recognizing that her son's personality strengths are different from hers.

Unmotivated children may seem easier to raise, but parents also struggle with these kids at times. They may not have the fortitude to stand up for themselves, withstand temptation, or push hard to complete a task. They're sometimes people-pleasers and may be easily directed in positive or negative ways, depending on who they're with. Interestingly enough, when it comes to defiance, these kids may be just as stubborn as strong-willed children.

One day, Marcus decides he doesn't want to play with George anymore. As Mom discusses the issue with Marcus, she discovers his frustration is motivating him to give up. In

In the same way that strong-willed children need stronger fences in their lives, unmotivated children often need the brush cleared off their paths of life.

fact, he does this regularly. If he doesn't get what he wants easily, he moves on to something else. Mom helps Marcus understand he should challenge George sometimes. She begins to equip her son with strategies and ideas and even coaches him to gently stand up for himself while George is over. Once Marcus puts his mom's ideas into practice, the boys play nicely more often, and Marcus has a good time.

In the same way that strong-willed children need stronger fences in their lives, unmotivated children often need the brush cleared off their paths of life. Children who tend to give up easily need help to see the path more clearly so they can take the steps necessary for success.

Strong-Willed Parents

Parents need to develop strong wills. It's not an option. Many strong-willed kids have weak-willed parents, allowing the children to become more selfish and demanding. Unmotivated children also need strong-willed parents to challenge them to succeed. Kids need parents who are willing to take a stand for what's right, demonstrate leadership, and set firm limits. They need moms and dads who will show them the path and encourage them to stay on it.

Unfortunately, some parents translate this mandate into a justification to rain anger down on their kids. Children need firmness, but don't think firmness is the same as harshness. Many parents confuse the two, but harshness damages relationships. Firmness sets down a boundary and lets children know that if it's crossed, a consequence will follow. Firmness holds a child accountable to take the next steps. Don't use your anger to overpower a strong will or to put a fire under an unmotivated child. It may work for a while, but in the end you'll lose closeness.

It Starts in the Heart

Strong-willed children need a solid, inner sense of direction to keep them on the right road. Those who are unmotivated need a passion to help them stay the course. Where does all this come from? It comes from the heart. So, wherever your child fits, you must start with the heart to see lasting change take place.

The disciple Peter was strong willed. He was quick to share his idea about building shelters for Elijah, Moses, and Jesus after the transfiguration (Matt. 17:4). He was the one who wanted to step out on the water to walk toward Jesus during a storm (Matt. 14:28). Peter needed a lot of redirection in his early life, but when it was time to pick someone to preach the sermon on Pentecost, Peter was chosen. Jesus was patient as he worked inside Peter's heart to build a man who could do the right thing, even under pressure.

> **MANY STRONG-WILLED KIDS HAVE WEAK-WILLED PARENTS, ALLOWING THE CHILDREN TO BECOME MORE SELFISH AND DEMANDING.**

When it came to pleasing his girlfriend, Samson was

unmotivated to remain righteous (Judg. 16:17). Although physically strong, he didn't have the internal stamina to withstand temptation, and tragedy struck his life. When God called Moses to lead the Israelites out of Egypt, he had to coax him along the way. Moses seemed rather unmotivated, content just to live on the backside of the desert. But God had another idea. Moses gave five excuses for not obeying God, and each time God revealed another answer, patiently guiding him to do what he was called to do (Ex. 3–4). Over time, Moses became a great leader, but God worked hard to bring him to that point. It took time to build in Moses' heart a confidence that God could handle any problem that might come.

SOMETIMES A MAJOR CRISIS CAUSES A CHANGE OF HEART, BUT MORE OFTEN IT HAPPENS OVER TIME THROUGH INTERACTIONS IN EVERYDAY LIFE.

Helping children develop a stronger will or redirecting their already strong will is a challenge in any home. The daily work of family life poses many opportunities to make changes. Instead of just reacting to the needs of the moment, parents would do better to identify the issues of the will and use a heart-based approach. Long-range solutions are always heart-related. Yes, you have to set limits and hold children accountable—but as you do, keep your focus on the heart. In the end, it's the heart change that your child needs to adequately guide the will.

Setting Limits for the Strong-Willed Child

The way God disciplined Saul of Tarsus redirected his intensity to something productive instead of destructive. God didn't just stop him from persecuting Christians. He redirected Saul's life goals so the same intensity Saul used to hurt others was applied to sharing Christ with people around the world. He changed his heart.

Sometimes a major crisis causes a change of heart, but more often it happens over time through interactions in everyday life.

A strong-willed child may object every time you give an instruction, and you may find it quite tempting to give in. After all, eventually the child discovers some logic that makes sense. Your child's lawyer-type approach has backed you into a corner, and you begin to feel like it would be wrong to stay the course. The child has successfully talked you into a compromise.

Now, it's important for parents to listen to their children. In fact, compromise can be a good thing in many situations. Asking children to propose an alternative solution helps them develop the ability to appeal graciously to authority. Parents should look for ways to incorporate children into the decision-making process.

But some parents have erred too far in that direction, and their children can't seem to follow any instructions without a dialogue. These parents feel as if they have

CONVERSATION CAN BE GOOD IN SOME CIRCUMSTANCES, BUT SOMETIMES STRONG-WILLED CHILDREN NEED TO JUST STOP RESISTING AND DO IT YOUR WAY.

to talk their kids into obeying, and children develop the belief that if they don't agree, they don't have to obey. Conversation can be good in some circumstances, but sometimes strong-willed children need to just stop resisting and do it your way.

Children who argue continually tend to value their own agenda above relationship. Their desires and getting what they want become the most important thing, revealing a heart-deep selfishness that needs to change.

If you find yourself in a pattern of never-ending spiral conversations, and your child is becoming more demanding and self-willed in this area, you need to develop a new routine. In a calm moment, have a sit-down meeting with your child and say, "We seem to have a problem when I give you an instruction you don't like. I appreciate your persistence and many of your ideas are good, but when I tell you to do something, that's not the time to argue. This is a heart problem. So from now on, when I ask you to do something, I want you to obey first; then we'll talk about it later. I want to see if you can accept my instructions and cooperate without arguing."

YOUR JOB IS TO TEACH YOUR CHILD WHERE LIMITS EXIST IN RELATIONSHIPS.

Your job is to teach your child where limits exist in relationships. As an adult, you know when challenging someone crosses the line of insubordination, but strong-willed children often lack the sensitivity to pick up on basic social cues that tell them when they've exceeded appropriate relational boundaries. Frustratingly, they often don't even take notice of the subtle correction cues you give, so you feel like you have to get angry or become blunt, cold, rude, or even mean to get the message across.

You don't have to be mean, but it is often necessary to exaggerate the cues. When a persistent child launches into his arguments, you might typically give a look that communicates, "I've heard enough." A sensitive person would catch that look and stop talking or change the subject. But your child doesn't get it, so you have to make the cues more obvious. Of course, some children see the cues but decide to ignore them. You can raise the awareness level and help children realize that you're not going to follow the same old script. You might say, "Son, I've given you my answer, and I want to be done with this conversation, but I feel like you're a big truck, and I'm being run over. It's time for you to stop trying to change my mind. We're done."

Many parents try to break the will. In fact you've probably heard the parenting proverb that goes like this: Break the will without breaking the spirit. This will only be productive if you have a heart-based approach to discipline, because stopping a child's determination forces her to reevaluate her values and priorities. You create a wall to block the child's will—but, at the same time, it's critical to feed the heart with new information and experiences. In this way, the walls you set up redirect a child's heart rather than just create a hurdle for her to overcome.

SOMETIMES PEOPLE WHO ARE UNMOTIVATED TO TAKE ACTION ARE QUICK TO COMPLAIN.

If behavior modification is the focus, however, determined children learn to get what they want. They discover ways to go through, over, around, or under your wall. It just takes time and a little creativity. The will is a good thing when it is directed by a wise heart, but a foolish heart creates a lot of pain for both the child and the parents.

Motivating the Unmotivated Child

The Bible tells us of people who needed a little extra motivation to get moving in the right direction. God often came alongside people such as Moses, Elijah, and Jacob to motivate them to take initiative when they might not have done so otherwise. In Judges 6, Gideon asked God questions, and it's as if God had to talk him into leading the people. He even used fleeces to make sure God wanted him to take leadership.

Sometimes people who are unmotivated to take action are quick to complain. It's much easier to criticize, whine, and point out the problem than to offer constructive advice and become part of the solution.

Eight-year-old Martin had a lot of complaints. Problems were never his fault, and he seemed to be able to point out others' weaknesses rather easily. Dad challenged his son one day by saying, "There are two kinds of people in the world: whiners and solvers. People in our office at work have complained for weeks that the office schedule disappears and people can't find it. Today I created a red folder for the schedule and a place to keep it. People are pleased because this will help solve the problem of the missing schedule." Dad was trying to get Martin to consider his own whining and complaining and teach him to take action instead.

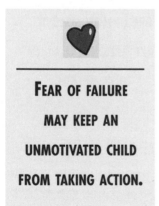

FEAR OF FAILURE MAY KEEP AN UNMOTIVATED CHILD FROM TAKING ACTION.

Even unmotivated people wrestle with issues and questions in their hearts, although you may not see it as clearly as in the strong-willed child. Some children process things more internally and aren't as transparent. These children appear compliant, allowing others to make decisions or take the lead, but their anger may be growing inside. The child may not know how to respond and choose to brood instead.

Fear of failure may keep an unmotivated child from taking

action. Some kids want everything perfect before they'll take the first step. Unlike the strong-willed child, who often learns by jumping in and making mistakes, the unmotivated child will hold back until more parts of the plan become obvious.

Hannah, age nine, is shy and rarely tries new things. She is hesitant to take on an instrument at school, doesn't want to play on a sports team, and won't attempt the extra credit project for science class. Hannah is not a behavior problem, but Mom is concerned because Hannah lacks initiative and isn't going anywhere in life.

Mom realized Hannah had a heart issue that was keeping her from many good things in life. Mom began to challenge her daughter in some positive ways. They talked about the benefits of initiative, and Mom required that her daughter do the extra credit assignment at school. Mom also shared Scripture with her daughter about people who stepped out of their comfort zone. Mom praised Hannah for small steps of initiative with her friends and at church. Mom knows that Hannah has a long way to go in this area, but she's not allowing the lack of behavior problems to prevent her from moving forward with her daughter.

Sometimes parents overlook the unmotivated child because she isn't causing any trouble, generally gets along with people, and appears easygoing. It may be more difficult to know what's going on in this child's heart, requiring extra work and effort. Give your children opportunity to test out new things without criticism. Failure is often a good teacher. Making mistakes is part of growth.

The Heart Guides the Will

When a child is strong willed and the heart is in the right place, God can do great things. But when a strong will crosses the line and becomes mean or takes advantage of others, it's wrong and needs correction. Similarly, when an unmotivated child's heart is in the right place, contentment results. However, when lack of motivation leads to irresponsibility, correction is necessary to bring attitudes and behavior back into line. Whether your child is strong willed or unmotivated or somewhere in between, what's important is the heart.

Prayer

Lord, teach me how to be strong willed with my children—not with harshness but with compassionate firmness. Give me insight into my child's motivation, and help me know where to set limits. Teach me how to direct my children in ways that are most productive. Help me see early when negative patterns are developing, and give me the motivation to hang in there when I feel like quitting. Amen.

Chapter 4

Do It Like You Mean It

The heart makes commitments, the will makes choices, and behavior is where it all comes out. The heart work, or lack of it, is revealed in behavior, what you see every day in your children's lives. Sometimes what's going on in the heart is a mystery, but behavior is always on display.

Jesus taught his disciples about the relationship between the heart and behavior in Matthew 12:33: "Make a tree good and its fruit will be good, or make a tree bad and its fruit will be bad, for a tree is recognized by its fruit." Jesus was pointing out the fact that a heart reveals itself in behavior. He also said, "The things that come out of the mouth come from the heart" (Matt. 15:18). If you watch children and listen to what they say, you'll learn more about what's going on deep inside.

Don't be fooled, however, by children who pretend to have their hearts in the right place. Sometimes behavior can mislead others. In speaking to the Pharisees in Mark 7:6, Jesus quoted Isaiah's words, saying, "These people honor me with their lips, but their hearts are far from me." Sometimes people modify their behavior just to hide what's really going on in their hearts.

All children display both good and bad behavior.

Sometimes kids do well at school or at their friends' homes. Parents get amazing compliments about how respectful, kind, and cooperative these kids are. But at home, disrespect, unkindness, and resistance dominate the same children's interactions. The inconsistency will eventually come together. Either children will grow more gracious at home, or they'll become more and more bold in their contempt for others. It all depends on what's going on in their hearts.

It's easy to fall into the trap of concentrating on behavior and missing the heart. After all, you can't see the heart, and working on it is more difficult. In a busy schedule, with all of the other stresses of life, many parents settle for outward conformity. Unfortunately, if not addressed, the heart problems grow and fester until they burst out in ways that shock parents.

Hypocrisy is behaving in a way that contradicts one's beliefs or feelings. When children act like they're obeying but turn around and grumble, complain, and do a half-hearted job, they're establishing a mask on the outside. This is dangerous—but the saddest thing is to watch parents excuse it with comments such as "Well, at least he's obeying" or "He's got a good heart." In reality, this kind of behavior indicates a decaying heart, with rebellion growing past dangerous levels.

> **BE CAREFUL NOT TO TEACH YOUR CHILDREN TO CLEAN UP THEIR BEHAVIOR ONLY TO COVER A DECAYING HEART.**

In Matthew 23:27–28 Jesus called the Pharisees "whitewashed tombs." To help passersby recognize a grave in that day, people would paint the rocks white. Tombs looked clean on the outside, but decay filled the inside.

Jesus knew the Pharisees focused on correct behavior and ignored the heart.

Be careful not to teach your children to clean up their behavior only to cover a decaying heart. Sometimes children will do what you ask just to get you off their backs or acquire some reward, but it's clear their heart isn't in it. This shows you must focus more on the heart.

When you see behavior problems, recognize that something deeper is going on. Target your discipline for the heart, because when the heart changes, kids make lasting adjustments in their lives. Jesus told the Pharisees how they could change: "You clean the outside of the cup and dish, but inside they are full of greed and self-indulgence.... First clean the inside of the cup and dish, and then the outside also will be clean" (Matt. 23:25–26).

TARGET YOUR DISCIPLINE FOR THE HEART, BECAUSE WHEN THE HEART CHANGES, KIDS MAKE LASTING ADJUSTMENTS IN THEIR LIVES.

Behavior Can Be a Tool for Heart Change

Although we must be careful not to focus on behavior alone, it's important to realize that sometimes behavior can change the heart. Ideally, we change from the inside out, adjusting the heart and giving God greater control, resulting in outward changes. But that isn't how it always works. In the Bible we read God's commands for behavior—and his expectation of obedience. These commands are important not just for their external value, but because obeying them changes us.

Sometimes people just don't feel like doing what's right.

Does that excuse their behavior? After all, they don't want to become hypocrites, and since they don't feel like doing what's right, why not continue to do the wrong thing until their hearts change? Of course the faulty reasoning here is obvious. Even if you don't feel like it, you need to do the right thing.

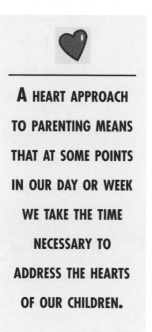

A HEART APPROACH TO PARENTING MEANS THAT AT SOME POINTS IN OUR DAY OR WEEK WE TAKE THE TIME NECESSARY TO ADDRESS THE HEARTS OF OUR CHILDREN.

Many of the chores your children do are likely a struggle for them. Unless your kids are exceptional, they get frustrated with work and view cleaning their rooms, washing the dishes, or raking leaves as an intrusion into their lives. In those moments, pray for heart change, talk about deeper issues, but continue to hold the line. Children who learn to work hard are eventually surprised by the amount of work they can do, but it takes time. Quite frankly, even parents get tired of chores and often do them out of duty. Even then, though, we can maintain positive attitudes because we know we're working for a greater good—the well-being of our families.

But how can we change the heart when we have to get the dishes done, clothes picked up, and get kids out the door to school? Heart work can seem elusive when you're faced with the urgency of daily life. Sometimes parents just have to do what needs to be done to keep things moving. But a heart approach to parenting means that at some points in our day or week we take the time necessary to address the hearts of our children. In the busier times, we make mental notes so we can develop a plan to reach down to the heart issues when the opportunity arises. But even on the run, many of the comments you make to your child reflect either a heart or a behavior approach to parenting.

Ten-year-old Jeffrey seemed irritated whenever Mom asked him to do something. She realized that his resistance was a pattern, likely indicating a heart problem. In the busyness of the morning one day, she took thirty seconds and stopped him in the hall. "Jeffrey, I'm going to give you some instructions this morning. I've noticed you often react unkindly to me when I do that. I'm concerned about the pattern I'm seeing, because it seems to indicate a problem in your heart. Would you please think about it?"

By confronting Jeffrey when she wasn't reacting to his disrespect, she made some progress. Jeffrey knew Mom wasn't just interested in getting the job done but was committed to helping him change his heart as well.

Behavior is important, and parents need to address the behavior problems they see. But that's only the beginning. We must also talk about heart issues and challenge our children to consider what's in their hearts.

Some children, however, seem to be doing pretty well. They follow instructions and seem to respond positively to life most of the time. How do we know if their hearts are in the right place or if what we see is just a big cover-up? When children are young, parents can get a pretty clear picture into the heart by watching behavior. Preschoolers and young elementary-age kids tend to be transparent. Their selfishness, pride, or dishonesty can be glaringly obvious.

As children get older, however, they may cover up problems and hold more in their hearts, be more secretive, and make it harder to know what's really going on inside. With these kids, we need to watch more closely for inconsistencies in behavior that may indicate a problem. Even if the

behavior isn't a concern, parents need to be diligent, looking for subtle cues. Pray that the Lord will make you
sensitive to the heart issues your child is wrestling with.
Pray for wisdom and discernment as you seek to uncover
what may be hidden. The Bible tells us two ways we can get
a picture into our kids' hearts: (1) listening and (2) looking
at what they treasure.

The Value of Listening

Jesus said, "Out of the overflow of his heart his mouth speaks"
(Luke 6:45); people talk about what's happening inside.
Parents can use this principle to look deeper into a child's
heart. In fact, both the things your child talks about and the
way those words are said become a gauge, giving you cues for
where to target your heart work.

"But my kids won't talk," some parents reply. It's surprising how many times we ask kids why they don't talk to their
parents and hear the same answer: "Because they don't listen to me." Yes, it's true some children confuse listening with
agreeing. They say to themselves, "My parents don't agree with
me—therefore they don't under-stand me or don't listen to what
I'm saying." These parents are often trying to listen, but aren't
persuaded to change their own opinions or decisions.

On the other hand, we find some parents really don't listen to
their children, whether they agree or not. They're irritated by the
illogic, different viewpoints, or

AS YOU LISTEN TO YOUR KIDS TALK, TRY TO DISCERN WHAT THEY BELIEVE THAT MAY BE DISTRACTING THEM FROM UNDERSTANDING THE TRUTH.

naïve opinions of their kids. Listening feels like torture as a child goes on and on about things that don't make sense to the parent. It's in these moments, however, that parents can learn a lot about a child's heart. Children may be wrong, but they're usually following some kind of internal logic.

As you listen to your kids talk, try to discern what they believe that may be distracting them from understanding the truth. Don't feel like you have to point it out on the spot. Take time to listen and make mental notes of errors in their thinking. Look for creative ways to help them understand truth more fully.

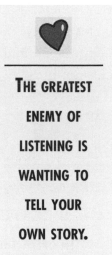

THE GREATEST ENEMY OF LISTENING IS WANTING TO TELL YOUR OWN STORY.

Proverbs 20:5 says, "The purposes of a man's heart are deep waters, but a man of understanding draws them out." The greatest enemy of listening is wanting to tell your own story. Be careful not to give your opinions too quickly. Kids shut down their hearts faster than a turtle can pull his head into his shell when they know sticking their necks out means having to listen to another lecture.

One dad realized his primary discipline strategy was forcing his daughter to listen to him when she made a mistake. Those lectures turned her off and she rarely wanted to spend time with him. He made some adjustments, abandoned the lecture approach, and used some heart-opening strategies. He focused more on his relationship with her by hanging out without an agenda, asking questions that didn't lead to a point, and complimenting her in areas of growth. Even when correcting he made shorter observations, gave clear instructions about what to do differently, and de-emphasized long diatribes about his philosophy of life. His daughter began to warm up to him again.

When the Millers and Turanskys were on a speaking trip and vacation in Hawaii, we visited the tide pools. The sea anemone reminded us of the sensitivity of many children's hearts. The fascinating little creature fastens itself to a rock with tentacles. Then, resembling a flower, it opens other tentacles widely, moving freely with the ocean current. If you take a stick and poke the center, the sea anemone quickly closes up tight. It takes time before the little creature will open up again.

AN ACCEPTING, SAFE, LISTENING EAR OFTEN OPENS THE HEART IN WAYS THAT NOTHING ELSE CAN.

The heart is like that. When prodded, it often contracts quickly. A harsh word, a sarcastic remark, or an angry jab may be the poke that hardens a child's heart. As parents begin to understand the heart, they realize how closed-off their child has become. Don't be discouraged. Although it takes time, you can still regain openness with your son or daughter. Much of the healing starts with listening.

An accepting, safe, listening ear often opens the heart in ways that nothing else can. As you listen to your child, you'll learn about dreams, goals, and commitments. Good or bad, time spent listening to your children gives you a greater sense of what's going on inside. Sometimes what you learn can show you what response is appropriate.

One mom of a fourteen-year-old boy said, "I realized that my son had been talking a lot about girls over the last couple months. My husband joked with him about it, and I could see that the teasing was closing him down, so my husband and I talked about it and decided to have more open, honest discussions with him. Our change in approach worked, and we've had some great talks together."

What Your Child Treasures

What are your kids interested in? What do they think about? Where do they spend their money? What do they want to do? Jesus said that "where your treasure is, there your heart will be also" (Matt. 6:21). Most of the time the activities our children choose indicate what they treasure.

Because the heart and behavior are closely linked, parents can look for things their kids can do that will encourage healthy heart change. Desires, hopes, dreams, and wishes start in the heart and then come out in a child's conversation. Eight-year-old Mike talked about becoming a pastor someday. He asked lots of questions about what pastors do and how he could become one. At home, however, he often got angry and hurt others with his words. He had a bad attitude toward his parents when they asked him to do something. And he spent a lot of time playing video games.

I (Scott) knew this was an opportunity to help him on a heart level. He desired to do something good but couldn't see the inconsistencies in his life that were preventing movement toward his goal. I pulled him aside one day for a talk. "Mike, I hear you want to become a pastor. That's a great goal. In fact, you'd make a great pastor because you're friendly and outgoing. But I see a couple of problems that might slow you down along the way. Would you like to know what those are?"

Mike's eyes grew large. "Sure."

"Well, I notice you have a hard time obeying your parents sometimes, and you have a problem with anger. Those two things will get in the way of your goals." We continued

to discuss the value of obeying and how peace was important for his heart so he could help others with their hearts.

Mike listened to what I had to say, and his parents
reported improvement at home. I also suggested Mike consider spending some time reading the Bible instead of
dedicating his time to video games. After all, if he wanted to
be a pastor, understanding the Bible was important.

Mike began to make life adjustments because I revealed
ideas that would bring his behavior more in line with his
heart longings. It made sense to him. He was ready to make
the changes. Children invest in the things that are in their
hearts. Part of our job as parents is to inspire our children
with a bigger vision for life, giving them something to set
their hearts on.

If the things your child values aren't helpful, look for ways
to limit them. One mom said, "We set a time limit on computer games because we saw they were consuming hours of
our son's time. It's helped us in two ways. First, he's started
building friendships with more children in the neighborhood.
We've enjoyed watching him develop these relationships. But
also we've been able to use the computer games as a privilege
to help motivate him to treat us kindly. He knows we don't
tolerate disrespect and that he may lose the little time he has
on the computer if he isn't careful."

Look for ways to guide your children into constructive and
helpful activities, hobbies, and relationships. Sometimes
you'll have to limit certain activities, but look for positive ones
to replace those you're taking away. Try to attract your children to good choices by providing opportunities they'd enjoy.
One dad gave his daughter a Christian-music sampler CD
because she believed all Christian music was boring. When
she heard some of the new songs, she realized many Christian
artists actually sang the kind of music she liked. Dad looked

for ways to encourage his daughter's interest in Christian music by sharing information about local concerts, special CD deals, and giving her music for her birthday.

Another dad felt uncomfortable about the amount of time his son was spending with neighborhood friends. When a Christian martial arts group started at church, he got his son involved. New friendships developed that replaced those from the neighborhood.

By adjusting what your children do, you can influence what they enjoy and eventually what they treasure. If they develop longings and desires to do the right thing, their choices will reflect those good values.

Sometimes simply providing different choices guides your child into more healthy heart situations, but other children seem to have a bent towards treasuring the wrong things. Or, they may want to spend hours in activities that aren't bad in themselves, but you know don't contribute to their maturity and growth. You may have to use a combination of approaches, including setting down some firm limits to guide your child in the right direction. That's part of

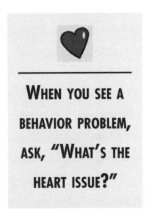

WHEN YOU SEE A BEHAVIOR PROBLEM, ASK, "WHAT'S THE HEART ISSUE?"

the hard work of parenting, but it's not optional. Be creative and look for alternatives, but recognize that, if a child isn't responding, you may have to provide parental control. Don't be afraid to take a stand to redirect your child into more healthy choices.

Challenge Behavior Using a Heart Approach

You may be wondering, "So what do I do when I see problems in my kids? Do I focus on the behavior or the heart issue?"

The answer is both. When you see a behavior problem, ask, "What's the heart issue?" Then develop a strategy that addresses both the heart issue and the behavior.

For example, let's imagine nine-year-old Samantha doesn't finish her homework assignments. Her teacher reports her work is sometimes sloppy and done only halfway; other times, it's not handed in at all. As we look at Samantha's life, we see she's also lazy with her chores and gives up easily when struggling with her friend.

The solution for Samantha will be two-sided. The behavior side may include setting up structures to help Samantha succeed. You could monitor her more closely and schedule a specific homework time, provide a quiet place for her to work undistracted, check her homework, and possibly even set up a reward system for when she finishes a job well.

Then, add a heart-focused side to the solution. Work on heart issues separate from schoolwork. Look for opportunities to build a vision for qualities such as thoroughness, diligence, responsibility, and self-control—and develop them.

The solution needs to acknowledge the behavior problem and work toward different actions. At the same time, the deeper heart issues need to be challenged. By taking a two-pronged approach, you can bring about lasting change while teaching appropriate behavior.

You work with your children's behavior every day. It's part of the job. As you continue to discipline for misbehavior and affirm positive actions, don't forget about the heart. Realize behavior indicates deeper things that need attention or encouragement. On the other hand, identify your kids' heart issues and look for ways to build patterns of behavior that target those heart concerns. By working on both behavior and the heart, you'll achieve maximum change in your children and contribute to their success both internally and externally.

Prayer

Father, as your child I want to serve you with all my heart, but for one reason or another I sometimes end up doing things that are wrong. Thank you for your forgiveness in my life. Please teach me how to look at my children's behavior and the things they say with discerning eyes; help me see their hearts. Lord, I ask you to reveal to me in clear ways the things I should do to influence my children to have hearts that serve you. Amen.

Part 2

Connecting with Your Child's Heart

A happy heart makes the face cheerful,
but heartache crushes the spirit.

PROVERBS 15:13

A Heart Story
from the Bible

Nehemiah lived in the palace in Susa, the beautiful capital of the Persian empire. He enjoyed life and had a good job working on the king's executive staff. But tonight, he couldn't sleep. His heart was wrestling with frustration.

Nehemiah was a man of action. He got things done. But sometimes accomplishing tasks wasn't easy, especially with a problem like this one. Earlier this evening, he'd talked with Hanani, a fellow Jew, who had just returned from Jerusalem. Nehemiah was always interested in hearing more about his homeland. It had been 140 years since Jerusalem had been destroyed and many of the people taken into exile. Some of their descendants now had returned.

Nehemiah had lots of questions. "How are the people doing in Jerusalem?" "What is the city like now?" "Are the people resettling and rebuilding there?"

As Hanani told story after story, Nehemiah's heart became more and more troubled. The people were suffering. They were being mistreated. He wanted to help, but what could he do for people who were so many miles away? He was frustrated, realizing the distance made assistance impossible. So Nehemiah prayed and asked God to help the people of Jerusalem.

A few days later, still troubled, Nehemiah was in the king's presence. It wasn't acceptable for a royal employee to look downcast or upset. The king paid people to be happy and make his life pleasant. As he looked at his trusted servant, the king could tell that there was a problem. "Are you sick, Nehemiah?"

"No, I'm not sick."

"If you're not sick, then there must be a problem in your heart. It's very unusual for you to be so down. What's going on?" The king liked Nehemiah, and seeing him suffer concerned him.

Nehemiah told the king what was in his heart. The more he listened, the more the king knew Nehemiah had a job to do. He knew that keeping Nehemiah in Persia wasn't the best thing. Yes, Nehemiah might continue to be a good employee, but his heart was elsewhere. The king was wise enough to release Nehemiah to go to his homeland to help the settlers. He supported Nehemiah with official letters, supplies, and money to accomplish the job.

Nehemiah was delighted. He wasted no time and was soon on his way. No doubt he was grateful for a leader who picked up on Nehemiah's emotional cues, willingly heard his heart, and responded to his needs.

(This story was taken from Nehemiah 1:1–2:10.)

Chapter 5

Emotions Have Feelings Too

T he heart is where we experience emotion. What people feel influences their decisions, reactions, and behavior. When a young man says to a woman, "I love you with all my heart," he means his emotions have helped guide his heart to commitment. But love isn't the only emotion in the heart. Anxiety, fear, and anger can turn a heart into a place of turmoil and distress; conversely, joy, peace, and love give a sense of well-being.

The Bible describes this emotional link. First Samuel 4:13 says that Eli's heart "feared" for the ark of God. Deuteronomy 1:28 says the spies who gave a bad report about the land discouraged the people's hearts. Psalm 61:2 speaks of an overwhelmed heart. In each case, emotions in the heart affected behavior.

It is true that many children decide what to do based on how they feel. They procrastinate because they feel unmotivated, react because they're angry, or give in to peer pressure to feel accepted. Through the everyday work of child training, parents help children learn that responsibility requires that we do things we don't feel like doing. Those who make decisions based only on how they feel often end up making poor choices.

A wise grandfather warned his grandchildren about falling in love. "You don't fall in love," he'd say. "You fall in ditches. You fall down stairs. You fall overboard. But you should plan your love life and choose carefully the person you're going to marry." This grandpa had a lot of wisdom. He understood that emotions are just one resource the heart contains for making decisions.

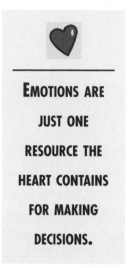

EMOTIONS ARE JUST ONE RESOURCE THE HEART CONTAINS FOR MAKING DECISIONS.

Nevertheless, the heart is where emotions are felt. Deep-seated needs are often experienced on an emotional level. Ultimately, God is the one who fulfills all of our needs, and he uses a number of tools to do so. God created the family to be a place where emotional needs are met. In fact, parents are a primary source for a child's emotional health, and how Dad and Mom relate to their children sets an important foundation.

Emotions Provide Information

People experience life on multiple levels. Our senses gather information and our brains process it. Feelings also give us cues and affect how we perceive life and interact with others. When understood, emotions become a valuable tool for gathering data and drawing conclusions. You've likely been in a situation where you felt that something wasn't right, even before you discovered what the problem was. Our emotions are like little sensors that can pick up nonverbal cues, attitudes, and tension in the air. Once your emotions signal there's a problem, then you can pursue a greater understanding of the situation.

Unfortunately, many people don't use their emotions in

this constructive way. When they feel a little uncomfortable, they just react emotionally, saying and doing counterproductive things. Robert, a father of three, realized this was true in his home. "I had no idea what was going on inside me, but I did know my children made me upset at times. I would tend to react harshly when I didn't even know the whole story. I spent some time evaluating my emotions, and now things are much different. When I feel uncomfortable or angry, I don't just react, but I try to figure out what's going on. I've learned more about my kids and we've grown closer together. I still have to confront them when they're doing the wrong thing, but I feel like I'm disciplining more effectively now."

Often, men have a harder time than women connecting emotionally with others. Emotional sensitivity is perceived as weakness in men, and even acknowledging feelings appears cowardly. Dads and husbands, however, find the work they do in this area pays huge dividends. Dads have a tremendous impact on their children's emotional well-being, and understanding emotions gives them greater effectiveness in their relationships. Charles began to learn more about his own feelings but realized he wasn't in the habit of sharing them with his son. One afternoon when his son was particularly helpful and pleasant he decided to take the risk. "Son, it sure makes me feel good when you're so helpful like this. It brings joy to my heart." Charles reported that the statement felt awkward, but he was rewarded with a big smile from his son. Dad recognized the value of communicating his emotions and began looking for ways to do it more.

Women, on the other hand, generally tend to have an easier time finding ways to emotionally connect with others. Many women are able to share feelings naturally in conversation and can imagine what others are feeling in a given situation. Emotional awareness is good, but some women let their emotions get the better of them and may respond solely on an emotional level. Of course, these generalizations aren't always true—warning us all to keep our emotions in balance.

If you tend to be emotional, be grateful. Learn to use your emotional sensitivity to connect with your child's heart.

EMOTIONS AREN'T AN ENEMY. THEY REVEAL VALUABLE INFORMATION ABOUT WHAT'S GOING ON IN THE HEART.

Consider your child's emotions and what they may be telling you. On the other hand, if you find feelings confusing and rather scary, take it slow, but begin to explore this new world that can bring energy and closeness into relationships. If you tend to shun emotions, you may want to use childrearing to help you grow in this area. Your children will benefit and so will you.

Working with Your Child's Emotions

Since the heart is where decisions are formed, commitments made, and beliefs established, your child's emotions become an opportunity for parenting. Many parents are afraid of their children's emotions and try to minimize them. It's true that one parental responsibility is to help our children manage their feelings effectively. But, contrary to popular belief, emotions aren't an enemy. They reveal valuable information about what's going on in the heart.

Many children express their emotions freely, giving parents obvious cues to guide their teaching and correction in this area. Some children, however, are more reserved, processing emotions internally without outbursts, tantrums, or crying episodes. Parents of these children must be even more aware of small cues, engage their children in conversation more often, and look for ways to help their children work through life's challenges without clogging their hearts with unresolved emotional residue.

Excitement uncovers what your children get passionate about. Joy reveals what your kids like. Anxiety discloses where your children feel weak or lack control. Sadness pinpoints pain in a child's life. And anger reveals unmet desires, a hurtful experience, or a violation of what they believe is right. Don't back away from your child's emotional intensity. Instead, figure out what else is going on in the heart.

Of course, that doesn't mean that a child who is upset should be allowed to be unkind or hurtful to others. Children who respond with meanness need discipline, but that's not all they need. They also need care and guidance to deal with their emotions in helpful and productive ways.

One mom told us how she began to work on emotion as well as behavior in her discipline. Her ten-year-old daughter was angry because her mom made her do her homework, wanted to check it, and required that she rewrite it. In the past, Mom's approach would be just to be firm and make her do it. This time, though, Mom decided not to be provoked by the angry outburst. While her daughter was still angry, they sat down at the table and Mom said, "Okay, I'm ready to listen."

"You shouldn't be telling me what to do. You're not my teacher. My teacher doesn't care if I turn it in that way."

Mom slowed down the process by suppressing her own desire to argue. She said, "So you're angry because I'm taking control of your homework."

"Yeah. It's my homework and I'm doing fine in this class."

"Okay, let me explain to you what I'm doing. It's true that I'm letting you manage yourself more, and most of the time you do pretty well. Last week though, you didn't turn in an assignment, so I felt like you needed some help. Furthermore, it looks like you've reduced the quality of your work. You used to be much more careful about doing a good job."

Her daughter was still angry, but Mom's refusal to become emotional herself and her willingness to listen produced some positive results. Mom used her daughter's emotion as a flag to identify a deeper issue. Her daughter believed Mom shouldn't be involved in schoolwork and the quality of work didn't matter. Mom was able to challenge both those ideas, but only because she took time to listen and discuss without intensity.

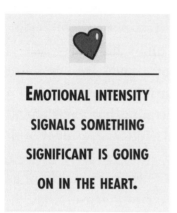

EMOTIONAL INTENSITY SIGNALS SOMETHING SIGNIFICANT IS GOING ON IN THE HEART.

"But I can't have a calm conversation with my kids," you might say. It's true that many families have developed such strong patterns of yelling, arguing, and fighting that change is a challenge. In those cases, larger doses of listening and even breaks in the dialogue that allow the child and parent to think for a bit before returning are necessary to get things back on track.

Emotional intensity signals something significant is going on in the heart. When life is moving at a calm, expected pace, emotions typically bounce around in a small range. It's when things are going exceptionally well or terribly awful or surprises happen (both good and bad) that children react emotionally. The intensity of the highs and lows varies from personality to personality.

Some parents are hesitant to move into this area of emotions because they're afraid it will open the door for their children to be rude, mean, and disrespectful. Children need firmness, and parental control is good for teaching self-control. The heat of the moment is rarely a good time to discuss emotions, but look for other times in life to help children process and understand how they feel.

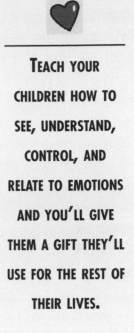

TEACH YOUR CHILDREN HOW TO SEE, UNDERSTAND, CONTROL, AND RELATE TO EMOTIONS AND YOU'LL GIVE THEM A GIFT THEY'LL USE FOR THE REST OF THEIR LIVES.

Kids long to connect with others, but many don't know how. Emotions are an essential tool for understanding and building relationships. Teach your children how to see, understand, control, and relate to emotions and you'll give them a gift they'll use for the rest of their lives.

Connecting Emotionally Opens Other Doors Too

One reason connecting emotionally is so important is that the heart is also a person's spiritual center; that's why God chooses to live there. It's also where we can impact our kids spiritually. When you connect with your children on an emotional level, they're more willing to listen to spiritual truth and less resistant to your leadership.

When we ask children who they talk to when they're upset, answers vary greatly. Some children talk to their friends, their parents, other family members, youth leaders, or teachers. And some children don't feel comfortable talking about their problems with anyone. Most children lack emotional coordination and are awkward about their feelings. It takes a patient parent to work with a child who's inexperienced in the emotion department. These kids need a parent willing to draw them out and pursue greater understanding.

In 1 Peter 1:22, Peter told believers how they can have closer relationships: "Now that you have purified yourselves by obeying the truth so that you have sincere love for your brothers, love one another deeply, from the heart." That's a helpful command for parents, too. We tend to want to keep things moving and keep our day organized and on track. Parents must continually evaluate their choices and decide what issues are most important in family life. As you make those tough trade-offs, be careful not to minimize the value of time well spent on relationship with your kids. Connecting emotionally takes time, but the reward of closer family relationships is great.

Prayer

Lord, emotions seem like a mysterious area. Please forgive me when I let my emotions get the best of me. Help me to see ways I can work with my child to teach valuable lessons about the heart. I pray, Lord, that you give my family a greater sensitivity to each other so we don't have to react as quickly and can process life with more wisdom. Teach me how to value my emotions as part of your creation and allow you to control how I use them. Amen.

Chapter 6

Turn on Their Heart Lights

Most parents love their children deeply (although day-to-day interaction may lead to fleeting second thoughts). But feeling love and communicating it are two different things. Many moms and dads assume their children know and feel their love, but kids need to have it communicated to them regularly. When children experience love from their parents, they feel worthy, significant, and acceptable and are able to withstand pressure and frustration more effectively. Also, when children *feel* the love of their parents, they're better able to understand God's love for them.

Emotionally connecting with your kids helps them experience love in a tangible way. They're then better able to sort through and respond appropriately to their own emotions, even negative ones. Anger, sadness, jealousy, fear, and a host of other emotions can leave kids confused. Those feelings can't be denied or ignored because they influence longings, desires, and commitments. A heart that feels loved and secure is better prepared to deal with these difficult aspects of life, but if a reservoir of unaddressed emotion keeps getting in the way, the decision-making process is clouded, and children have a hard time making wise choices.

Some parents believe that closeness and feeling loved spring naturally from the parent-child relationship. One homeschooling mom told us, "I came to the striking realization that, although the school time we spent together was valuable, I wasn't connecting emotionally with my kids. I thought that because I was with my children for hours every day, we'd feel closer. It wasn't happening. In fact, the work of homeschooling seemed to create more tension and distance in our relationships.

"I realized I had to do more than teach them during the day to make the connection. I'm tired when school is over and I often want to rest, thinking my job with my kids is done because I finished the day's lesson plan. I realized that was a mistake. I added fun times with my kids both inside and outside of school, and I saw the change in my children. We not only felt closer, but I noticed they were more cooperative with their schoolwork."

Parents must maintain a balance as they work with their kids. Firmness, confrontation, and correction in a child's life are tools that God uses to address heart issues. You won't get very far, however, by simply telling your children the right thing to do. Remember that a child can only take as much pressure as the relationship can withstand. Those who apply force without relationship end up with angry and rebellious kids.

Jesus was a great example of leaving behind the agenda to care for people and connect with their hearts. He rebuked Martha for her busyness and affirmed Mary for just sitting with him (Luke 10:38–42). Another time, when Mary put perfume on Jesus' feet and wiped them with her hair, Jesus defended her against Judas's accusations (John 12:3–8). At his last supper with his disciples, Jesus illustrated servanthood by getting up and washing the disciples' feet (John 13:1–5). As you imagine Jesus ministering in these and other situations in the Gospels, you can picture his amazing ability to connect with people emotionally.

Paul told Christians in God's church to "rejoice with those who rejoice; mourn with those who mourn" (Rom. 12:15). Emotionally connecting with others is important in God's family and essential in the earthly family as well.

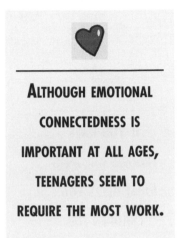

ALTHOUGH EMOTIONAL CONNECTEDNESS IS IMPORTANT AT ALL AGES, TEENAGERS SEEM TO REQUIRE THE MOST WORK.

Although emotional connectedness is important at all ages, teenagers seem to require the most work. Parents are often appalled by the crazy ideas their teens have and the intensity their kids use to resist parental guidelines. Just when you thought your job as a parent was winding down, it becomes more intense, putting further pressure on the relationship. When you initiate closeness with your teen, you're sometimes rebuffed and rejected, making the challenge even more difficult—but continually pursuing your children produces lasting results.

Many a tired parent asks, "Why do I want closeness with my child anyway?" Distance from children can even seem welcome sometimes. Some parents are frustrated with their role and eager for relief. One mom even believed distance was healthy: "Aren't teens supposed to hate their parents to prepare them for the upcoming separation and independence they need?"

This kind of attitude hinders a parent's effectiveness. Teenagers may reject closeness with parents sometimes, but adolescence is when they need the relationship the most.

New values, decisions, and difficult choices require wisdom that the teen doesn't have yet. Young people need insight and guidance that parents can give them.

Teens are much more likely to accept teaching from their parents when they have a close relationship. Continuing to work on emotional closeness is foundational to significantly affecting your teenager's choices and lifestyles. Teens may try to push you away. Don't let their immaturity discourage you. Consistently look beyond their actions to see the needs in their hearts.

IF YOU HAVE TROUBLE KNOWING WHAT HELPS YOUR CHILDREN FEEL LOVED, ASK THEM.

Emotionally connecting with your children isn't done just so you can all feel good. Connecting with your son or daughter emotionally softens hearts and prepares the way for much of the hard work of parenting, making it more tolerable and perhaps even enjoyable.

How to Connect Emotionally with Your Kids

You must be proactive to maintain closeness with your children. Start by asking yourself the important question, "How does my child like to be loved?" Your son may enjoy cuddling, a back rub, or a big hug, because physical touch communicates love to him. Your daughter may thrive on affirmation, because she longs for Mom or Dad's approval. Another child may just enjoy talking and being with you, playing a game, reading a book, or watching TV together. Each child is different. If you have trouble knowing what helps your children feel loved, ask them. They often have insights that get you thinking in the right direction.

Closeness with children is important in and of itself, but it doesn't stop there. Once you open a window of emotional closeness, you earn the right to communicate more directly to your children's hearts. They're more willing to hear you out or enter into conversation about sensitive issues. Be cautious, though. An open heart is a fragile place. Some parents go in with swords and clubs where tweezers are needed. A heart closes much faster than it opens, so be careful with the opportunities you have.

One mom told us this story: "Every time I asked my five-year-old, Jason, to do anything, he resisted me. He argued, complained, and had a bad attitude. I wasn't getting anywhere with him, and our relationship seemed to be getting worse. Then he got sick. It was just the flu for a couple of days, but during that time he wanted me to hold him and cuddle with him. He just seemed to soak in the affection. I felt like we connected on a deeper level during those moments.

"After he was well again, he seemed to be more responsive to me for about a week. Then old patterns returned. I decided to try something. One afternoon I asked him if he'd like me to rock him in our rocker. Surprisingly, he said yes. For about twenty minutes he seemed to cherish the attention. Amazingly, he was more responsive to me the rest of the day. In fact, I felt more nurturing to him as well, and I'm sure that came across in my attitude toward him. I think we both need for me to hold him often. The cuddling contributes to greater cooperation between us."

Some parents have a natural ability to communicate effectively. Often in a family, one parent finds this easier than the other. Learn from each other what works, and respect the communication skills each parent has. Over the years, Carrie and I (Scott) have gone back and forth with the ability to get close to our kids. Sometimes I can connect with one of our

kids in a special way, but when I turn around and try to connect with another child, it just doesn't seem to work. Carrie
then amazes me with her combination of tact and boldness to
communicate an important truth. It just further confirms the
fact that kids aren't cookie dough, waiting to be pressed into
shape. The family dynamic is always in flux and we, as parents, must be ready to adjust.

**THE INTANGIBLE
GIFTS WE GIVE
OUR CHILDREN
USUALLY TOUCH
THE HEART MORE
EFFECTIVELY
THAN THE
TANGIBLE ONES.**

In the continuing search for practical
suggestions for achieving emotional connectedness, we've devised several
categories. View these as gifts you give
to your child. Sometimes these gifts are
tangible, like a toy, new clothes, or an
unexpected activity. However, unless
the gift matches a desire in their hearts,
children may not appreciate the gesture
of kindness.

Furthermore, some children are
demanding, always asking for more and
wanting things they can't have. At those
moments, it's tempting for parents to
give in for the sake of relationships.
That's rarely helpful; instead, those gifts
tend to feed an indulgent attitude and compromise standards
and values. When children are demanding, they need more
limits and more "no" answers to their requests.

But even these children need gifts of love. The intangible
gifts we give our children usually touch the heart more effectively than the tangible ones. Kids need gestures of kindness,
such as making their favorite dinner or giving a back rub.

Here are eleven categories of heart gifts you can give to
your children. Not all work with every child, but with a little
experimentation, you'll find ones that will connect with your

kids in significant ways. These ideas are just meant to get you started. Create a list that contains ways to connect emotionally with each child. Doing these things one-on-one helps tremendously, so plan some time with each child alone. You may want to set a goal of ten minutes a day or an hour or two a week. Undoubtedly your life situation and child's needs will help dictate what's reasonable for you, but remember that it's always a challenge to move from the status quo. Stretch yourself in some new ways, and you and your child will both benefit.

1. *Talking.* Tell stories about interesting things that are happening in your life. Children often like to hear you describe events from your own childhood. Don't feel like you have to tie a lesson into the story. Just tell it to them as if you were relating the details to a friend. Talk about their childhood, too. Kids love to hear about what they were like as babies and young children.

2. *Listening.* Your kids have stories, too. Ask questions and take an interest in their activities and their day. Ask them about favorite things they enjoy and let them share their opinions. Once they start talking, draw them out with more questions. Ask your child for advice and genuinely listen.

3. *Touching.* A hug or a gentle hand on a shoulder communicates warmth and love. Try moving out of your comfort zone by giving a hug when you otherwise might not. With practice, you'll learn how and when to touch your child.

4. *High-energy activities.* Kids love excitement. Play games with them. Preschoolers love hide and seek. Play with lots of energy and even silliness. Older children often enjoy interactive, fast-paced card games. Some children prefer to watch and others prefer to play. Look for exciting activities to enjoy together.

5. *Interests.* What does your child like? Children may be interested in animals, airplanes, cooking, or race cars. Look for ways to share your child's interests. They may not be your favorite, but they become bridges to a greater sense of closeness.

6. *Special treats.* Gifts of love don't have to cost a lot of money. Buy your son's favorite ice cream or pick up some corn on the cob because you know he likes it. Give your daughter the fancy little flashlight that came in the mail. Stop on the way home for a milk shake or check out a book from the library you know your child will enjoy.

COMMUNICATE GRATEFULNESS AND AFFIRM GROWTH IN CHARACTER YOU SEE IN YOUR CHILD.

7. *Partnering.* Find a service project you can do together. Team-teach Sunday school, make a meal and deliver it to a friend who's sick, visit with nursing-home residents, or fix a car. Find a task and work at it together as teammates. Consider allowing the child to lead and you be the assistant.

8. *Praise.* Offer genuine praise for a job well done. Communicate gratefulness and affirm growth in character you see in your child. If someone gives you a good report about your child, pass on the praise. Admire something about your child and communicate it.

9. *Fun.* Be silly, tell jokes, or wrestle with your kids. Be playful. Use squirt guns, run around the house, play it up, and generate a fun moment.

10. *New times in a child's life.* The first day of school, the trip to the orthodontist for braces, setting up a bank account, a girl's first period, or a first airline flight all can set the stage

to connect emotionally. Be there and available to share the moment.

ENJOY YOUR KIDS AND HAVE FUN WITH THEM.

11. Traumatic events. A bad grade, an unfair teacher, a trip to the emergency room, or the death of a pet all provide opportunities to develop closeness. Remember that the most important thing isn't fixing the problem, it's restoring the heart.

In short, enjoy your kids and have fun with them. Take an interest in their lives. If you don't feel like it, do it anyway. Your kids need your playfulness, love, affection, and joy. When you give to your kids, you contribute to their well-being and your family's strength. Yes, it's sacrifice, but the time you put in now will go a long way toward reducing friction when it's time to confront or discipline.

One mom said, "My ten-year-old son loves it when I run my fingers through his hair. He's liked that for years, and it became a special way for me to connect with him. I can tell he tends to act out more and resist me when I'm not spending quality time with him. I continually must remind myself to touch, play with, and listen to him."

If you don't feel like connecting emotionally with your children, take a look at your own heart. It's always easier to connect when emotions coincide with decisions we make, but that's not always how life happens. You already do a lot of things you don't feel like doing because you've made the commitment. Your heart is fueled by several factors; emotion is only one of them. Don't let the lack of positive feelings weaken your heart commitment to your children. They need you. When you use conviction to motivate your behavior, an amazing thing happens: Your emotions often follow.

Sometimes cultural differences affect the emotional connections in a family. One man told us, "I'm in an accountability group with some other men. One guy is from Puerto Rico, and he hugs and kisses his kids all the time, even as teenagers. I wasn't brought up that way. In our family we rarely say 'I love you,' let alone show any affection. When I was having trouble with my sixteen-year-old son, my friend suggested I be more affectionate. That was hard, but I tried it.

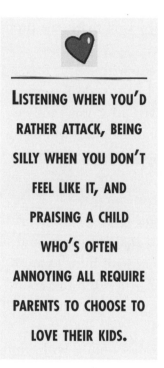

LISTENING WHEN YOU'D RATHER ATTACK, BEING SILLY WHEN YOU DON'T FEEL LIKE IT, AND PRAISING A CHILD WHO'S OFTEN ANNOYING ALL REQUIRE PARENTS TO CHOOSE TO LOVE THEIR KIDS.

"At first, I just started using words. Then, in a kind of teasing way, I began to touch my son, giving him a little squeeze on his shoulder, a one-armed hug, just to test the waters. He didn't pull back from me like I thought he would, so one day when I was leaving for work, I gave him a hug. He hugged me back. I was surprised. I've got a long way to go in this area, but I think I'm developing a new way of saying 'I love you' to my son."

Almost always, parents find emotional connectedness stretches their comfort zone. Listening when you'd rather attack, being silly when you don't feel like it, and praising a child who's often annoying all require parents to choose to love their kids. Love is work; that's true in marriage and it's true with children. But that loving work produces opportunities for closeness, spiritual connection, and heart change.

Look for ways to give to your kids, even if they don't deserve it. Firmness is important, but so is grace, so keep a careful balance. Often, giving a little extra heart gift regularly increases cooperation and responsiveness to your leadership.

Prayer

Lord, stretch me in new ways. I ask that you reveal things I can do to connect with my child. Sometimes I feel like we're so similar, and other times we seem miles apart. Please help me know how we can connect and then provide the time and energy I know I'll need to do it. Allow me to be a student of my child and learn new ways to connect on a deeper level. Amen.

Chapter 7

Avoiding Congestive
Heart Failure

Connecting with your children's hearts contributes to their emotional health. Part of your parenting work is to help your children understand emotions and process them appropriately. Children need to know how to handle disappointment, guilt, anger, anxiety, grief, and a host of other emotional challenges they face.

One sign of an emotionally healthy person is the ability to recover more quickly from upsetting experiences. I'm sure you know people who can stew for days when they're angry. God designed the heart as a place where emotions are experienced and then released. When people harbor negative feelings, the heart gets congested, leaving emotional residue. Healthy people experience emotions, benefit from them, release them, and move on. Emotionally unhealthy people overreact, mull over their feelings for long periods, and take longer to bounce back. Congestive heart failure is not just a physical problem in our society, it's also a spiritual problem in many relationships.

Take grief as an example. Grief can range from intense reaction to a deep loss to the minor disappointments of one's day. Maria, now a mom, told a story of when she was eight:

"Our cat, Sheba, was very sick and my mom took him to the vet to be put to sleep. I had such a hard time losing my cat; Sheba had been in our family since I was a baby. I remember getting mad at my parents. I accused them of killing Sheba. I know that wasn't fair, but I was upset, and my heart hurt so much. If I would have known then what I know now about grief, I'm sure I would have handled it differently. I didn't know how to respond to the pain my heart felt."

On the other hand, some children have a hard time knowing the difference between major and minor losses. One dad used a point system to discuss disappointment with his son. "On a scale of one to ten, with ten being the very worst and one being minor disappointment, I asked him to give me an example of a ten. He said he felt like a ten when Grandma died. I then asked him for an example of a one, and he mentioned having to play catcher instead of first base on his Little League team.

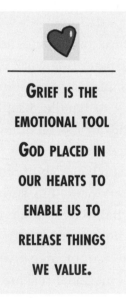

GRIEF IS THE EMOTIONAL TOOL GOD PLACED IN OUR HEARTS TO ENABLE US TO RELEASE THINGS WE VALUE.

"I then suggested that sometimes it seemed he gives an 'eight' reaction to a 'two' kind of problem. I used the conversation to help him see that maybe he was overreacting to some of life's challenges and working himself into unnecessary intensity. I used the point system over several days to help him evaluate some of his disappointments and his reactions to them."

Teaching children how to grieve is important for their emotional health. Parents might consider this sensitive part of a child's life when a loved one dies, but what happens when your son loses the soccer championship or your daughter is left out of the slumber party? Those are also significant opportunities to help your children learn to process their emotions.

Grief is the emotional tool God placed in our hearts to enable us to release things we value. For some, that's more difficult than for others. If you say to your son, "Stop crying like a baby," you miss an opportunity to teach him about grieving. We all invest our emotions to varying degrees. The child who's disappointed because he can't go camping on the weekend may have a hard time releasing that desire. In fact, he may react in anger to everyone around, forcing you to exert some discipline. In your firmness, look for ways to acknowledge the loss and to comfort him in the process. You might say, "I know you're angry because you're disappointed that you can't go on the camping trip, but the way you're handling it is wrong. I'm sorry you're feeling bad, and maybe I can help you with that, but not while you're being hurtful to others. So, you're going to have to think about it in the hall for a while before you come back and talk to me some more."

A child's heart can be a confusing place. Many different things are all happening at the same time. New information is added every day, requiring shifts in perspective and baffling even the most healthy or intelligent children. Having their deep emotional needs met allows kids to think more clearly.

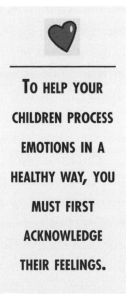

TO HELP YOUR CHILDREN PROCESS EMOTIONS IN A HEALTHY WAY, YOU MUST FIRST ACKNOWLEDGE THEIR FEELINGS.

The story of Elijah illustrates this well. In 1 Kings 19 the prophet was discouraged and moping around, feeling sorry for himself. Elijah believed he was the only prophet left in Israel, and the more he thought about it, the bigger the problem seemed. Elijah grew fearful and ran for his life. God knew Elijah's thoughts and emotions had gotten the best of him, but God didn't correct or rebuke him. Rather, he let him sleep and took care of him for several days so that Elijah could emotionally recover from the intense time of ministry he'd experienced. Only after Elijah was stronger did God reveal the truth to him: "I have seven thousand who have not bowed the knee to Baal" (v. 18). Before God could help Elijah change his heart, he first dealt with the emotions that were preventing clear thinking.

Parents Are Personal Trainers for Emotional Health

To help your children process emotions in a healthy way, you must first acknowledge their feelings. In many families, emotions are stifled and ignored. Angie told us her story: "In my home growing up, we didn't talk about emotions at all. In fact, the only emotion I can remember was anger. My dad would blow up, and the explosion would send us all scurrying to our rooms. There was never any resolution. We all waited for the energy to die down, but the effects lingered on. Now I see the same pattern playing out in our home. I get angry with my kids and I don't know how to end it. I don't like what I'm seeing, so I'm learning to be less intense to start off with. Then I'm looking for ways to come back and talk with them afterward."

Children often don't understand what's going on in their hearts. With young children, you might start teaching about three basic emotions: sad, mad, and glad. Ask kids, "How can you tell when a person is sad?" Let them talk about the visual cues we receive from others that tell us they're upset. Raising their awareness in this way gives children a greater emotional vocabulary. They'll be able to recognize these emotions in themselves, and the greater understanding will help them process what they're feeling.

Sometimes, when you try to talk to children about what they're feeling, they start talking about the issue. You say, "It sounds like you're angry with your brother."

Your child responds, "He took my shirt without even asking."

In those moments, you'll likely talk about the shirt issue, but then go back and talk about the emotion as well. "It seems when you get upset you spend a lot of energy feeling angry instead of spending some of that energy solving the problem. It looks to me like you're

WHEN CHILDREN BEGIN TO UNDERSTAND THEIR OWN EMOTIONS, THEY DEVELOP GREATER SENSITIVITY TO OTHERS, LEARN TO SEE HOW THEY'RE FEELING, AND THEN RESPOND IN HELPFUL WAYS.

pumping up your anger and it's making you an unhappy person. Your brother was wrong, and we need to confront him, but you're letting that problem hurt you even more by your reaction. It would be better to deal with it and move on instead of churning about it."

Some children have a rather narrow repertoire of emotional tools. They tend to express anger whenever they experience any negative emotion. When they're sad, they get angry. When they're afraid, they show anger. When they're disappointed, they take it out on others by getting mad. Other children withdraw and become depressed in response to negative feelings. By talking about other emotions, many children are then freed to experience them in more constructive ways.

When children begin to understand their own emotions,

they develop greater sensitivity to others, learn to see how they're feeling, and then respond in helpful ways. The emotionally illiterate person tends to react poorly to others' emotions, taking the cues as a personal attack. So when Mom is disappointed, her daughter starts defending herself. When Dad is grumpy, his son retaliates. Teach your children to see emotions in others, and they'll develop a greater empathy and relational maturity.

Emotions always indicate something going on inside. When six-year-old Paul is overly excited, he becomes annoying. He's actually experiencing a positive emotion, but he handles it poorly and then doesn't understand why others are upset with him. Mom has learned to recognize this exuberance and talk to him about it. "Paul, I want you to come over here and hold my hands. I can tell you're excited right now. It looks like you're having fun. I like the way you're happy a lot of the time. But when you get in people's faces like that, or you start teasing, it's not fun for others. I want you to think about that. If it continues, I'm going to call you over and have you sit for a minute to help you see what's happening."

Mom was firm, but she gently helped her son understand the emotions that were driving his annoying behavior.

Keep in mind that if patterns have accumulated over a long period, you may not see change quickly—but don't give up. Some parents have told us they've used these ideas with their adult children after years of walls and emotional pain and have finally seen miracles take place.

Old Patterns Get in the Way

Some ways parents relate to their children work against emotional connectedness. It's hard work looking for those special moments. Be careful not to undermine your own efforts with actions that close your child's heart, such as the following:

1. *Using anger as discipline.* Angry responses, sarcasm, and mean words may seem justified at the moment, but they do more harm than good. Anger builds walls in family life. Too many parents use intensity to get things done, trading closeness with their children for being on time or getting the house clean. Firmness is important with children, but harshness hinders closeness.

Some parents believe they have to get angry to get their kids moving. That's true in many families—but that's often because parents have trained their children to respond to anger as the indicator that they mean business.

Children are smart, and they learn where a parent's "action point" is. If you habitually use anger as the cue you're serious, your kids will delay until they see your intensity rise. One way to move away

BE CAREFUL THAT, IN YOUR DESIRE TO SOLVE PROBLEMS, YOU DON'T LOSE THE EMOTIONAL CONNECTEDNESS THAT COMES THROUGH VULNERABILITY.

from anger in relationships is to move to the correction step more quickly and use consequences besides anger to discipline children. (For more on this topic, see our book *Home Improvement: Eight Tools for Effective Parenting* [Cook, 2004].)

2. *Focusing on problem-solving instead of empathy.* Another hindrance to deeper relationships is to problem-solve too early instead of showing empathy. When children begin to open up emotionally, they reveal problems so obvious that you may have trouble resisting the urge to fix them. Be careful that, in

your desire to solve problems, you don't lose the emotional connectedness that comes through vulnerability. Many a hurt has come when a child shares a problem and, instead of caring and comforting, the parent moves into problem-solving mode. Kids need advice and counsel, but they also need love and care.

3. *Lecturing.* This is another common pitfall that prevents emotional growth. Just because you want to lecture doesn't mean your child is ready to learn. Some children shut down and just tolerate a lecture, missing much of the content. Teaching is valuable, but kids need parents to be creative and sensitive for them to learn life lessons.

PARENTS WHO USE CHILDREN'S MISTAKES AS EXAMPLES OF WHAT NOT TO DO OFTEN GIVE THE IMPRESSION THAT THE CHILD CAN'T MEASURE UP—WHICH, OF COURSE, DECREASES THE CHILD'S WILLINGNESS TO OPEN UP.

4. *Criticizing.* Too much criticism also hinders emotional connectedness. In love, parents often establish high standards of excellence. You want your children to work a little harder, make wiser choices, and exert more self-control. It may seem that the fastest way to change children is to point out when they miss the mark, but efficiency may miss effectiveness. Children often perceive parents as critical in these moments and have a hard time believing that anything they do is right. Parents who use children's mistakes as examples of what not to do often give the impression that the child can't measure up—which, of course, decreases the child's willingness to open up.

When Parents Struggle with Emotions

"How can I help my son deal with his anger when I can't even deal with my own?" We've heard that question over and over. It's a good question. The answer is we must make emotional health a family goal, something we're all working on. In fact, your vulnerability, willingness to admit when you're wrong, and desire to change contribute to a positive atmosphere where children learn that healthy people aren't perfect—they're just growing. Modeling growth is more valuable than appearing perfect.

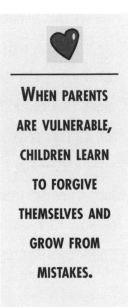

WHEN PARENTS ARE VULNERABLE, CHILDREN LEARN TO FORGIVE THEMSELVES AND GROW FROM MISTAKES.

One family had a meeting they called the "Feeling Meeting" every week for six weeks. As they talked about some of the times people got upset that week, they were surprised at how often they had misread each other. "I thought you were angry with me by the way you were talking, but it sounds like you were upset because of what happened at school." And, "When you were disappointed because I told you you couldn't go to that movie, you huffed and stomped off. How do you think I should respond to you in that situation, since the actions are wrong, even though I can understand your feelings?" These conversations increased this family's awareness of each other, and they learned some valuable new ways to relate.

In these kinds of meetings, both kids and parents learn a lot about each other and about how to read and relate to those outside the family as well. In moments of vulnerability we see our own weaknesses and are able to work on them. When you fail, admit it. Model humility as you grow. Require the same from your kids. When parents are vulnerable, children learn to forgive themselves and grow from mistakes.

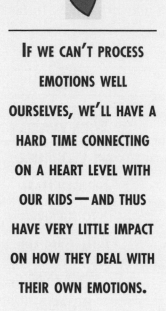

IF WE CAN'T PROCESS EMOTIONS WELL OURSELVES, WE'LL HAVE A HARD TIME CONNECTING ON A HEART LEVEL WITH OUR KIDS — AND THUS HAVE VERY LITTLE IMPACT ON HOW THEY DEAL WITH THEIR OWN EMOTIONS.

Patty has six children, requiring all her organizational skills to keep things running smoothly around their home. Before she had kids, she managed an office staff of forty employees. She did it well, and many people admired her and came to her for advice. But that was nothing compared to running her household. One of Patty's daughters, nine-year-old Ruthann, struggles with feelings of inferiority. She lacks confidence and rarely tries new things.

For years, Patty tried to help her daughter by telling her how to be strong and more courageous, even having her memorize Bible verses on that theme—but she saw very little progress in Ruthann until vacation Bible school one summer. Patty overcommitted herself, running the children's program at their church. It taxed her so much she couldn't keep up. She asked Ruthann for help, and the girl rose to the occasion. During that week, Patty learned that admitting her own weakness allowed her daughter to be strong. Patty continued to share her weaknesses with Ruthann over the next several months, and her daughter willingly took on new challenges. Patty's vulnerability gave her the opportunity to connect with Ruthann's heart, and she enjoyed watching Ruthann's character develop over the next few years.

Spend some time reflecting on your own emotions. How are they affecting *your* heart? Do they get in the way, or are you able to use them successfully to help you? Emotions are a gift from God. They provide a sixth sense for picking up cues in your environment. They add spice to life and provide connecting points with other people.

If we can't process emotions well ourselves, we'll have a hard time connecting on a heart level with our kids—and thus have very little impact on how they deal with their own emotions. Processing emotions well is an important lifestyle lesson children learn in a family.

I, Scott, like to tell kids the story of the clogged sewer pipe in the basement. One day, the pipe got stopped up, and all the drainage from the whole house backed up and came out the downstairs toilet because it was the lowest drain in the house. What a mess! The plumber came and opened the clean-out valve that led to the street. It was flowing well, revealing that the problem was somewhere farther up in the house. He ran his plumber's snake up the drain until, whoosh, the sewage ran smoothly again.

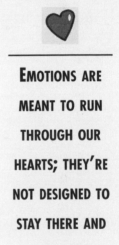

EMOTIONS ARE MEANT TO RUN THROUGH OUR HEARTS; THEY'RE NOT DESIGNED TO STAY THERE AND BUILD UP.

Emotions are meant to run through our hearts; they're not designed to stay there and build up. When we let them grow and intensify in our hearts, they back up, and all kinds of junk comes out into our lives.

An emotionally healthy child is able to process feelings without letting them bottle up or explode. That often takes years of training, but the work you do as a parent contributes to that growth. So, don't give up. Hang in there. Ask God for new strategies for connecting with your son or daughter emotionally. It's an essential part of the process of discipline and will help you reach your child's heart.

Prayer

Lord, please teach me how to be comfortable with my own emotions and those of my children. Free me from the need to respond negatively to the intensity I see sometimes. Please give me insight into my children and the wisdom to draw them out in helpful ways. Help me know when to draw the line on inappropriate behavior in a way that touches the heart as well. Amen.

Chapter 8

Making the Connection

Connecting with your child's heart requires creativity and experimentation. You're probably already learning some unique things about each of your children. Some parents feel overwhelmed at what needs to change and appreciate specific ideas that answer the question, "Where do I start?" This chapter gives you two important issues to consider as you try to connect with your child's heart.

Communication Tips

Communication is at the center of all relationships. Love is communicated in many ways, and people give and receive love differently. Talking and listening become essential tools for connecting with others and are vehicles that help us move deeper in relationships.

Five levels of communication provide opportunities for increased closeness in family life. Each level serves an important role for growing deeper. If tension and stress dominate your relationship with your child, start working through these communication levels and you'll begin to see significant change take place.

Level 1: Greeting

Greetings are the oil that keeps relationships cordial. "Hi!" "How are you doing?" "Good morning!" "How's it going?" If you want to move deeper, this is a great place to start. Many parents miss one of the easiest ways to begin connecting.

HUGGING YOUR CHILDREN AS PART OF A GREETING OR WELCOMING THEM TO BREAKFAST IN THE MORNING MAKES AN IMPORTANT STATEMENT ABOUT THE VALUE OF YOUR RELATIONSHIP.

Sometimes family life becomes very familiar, and people stop greeting or acknowledging each other. Hugging your children as part of a greeting or welcoming them to breakfast in the morning makes an important statement about the value of your relationship. These small acts of graciousness often open doors for greater closeness. If you feel like emotional walls have built up over time, this first step of graciously acknowledging your child may open the door for deeper communication.

Level 2: Facts

Exchanging information about our lives helps people know what's going on and contributes to a sense of connectedness. Talk about the weather, the news, a sports update, or a fun story about your life to get things started. As you go through your day, think of a couple of interesting things you could share with your child.

Most parents wish their children would share more information. Sometimes children are hesitant to share because parents become critical or see it as an opportunity to lecture. "That reminds me ..." Be careful to take an interest in your children's lives simply to learn what's going on and get to know them better.

You might ask, "What was the highlight of your day?" or "What was something you saw or experienced that was interesting today?" If your child doesn't respond with information easily, avoid typical questions such as, "How was your day?" Instead, be specific: "What did you do in gym class today?" Try to be creative to motivate your kids to share some facts about their lives.

Level 3: Opinions and Judgments

This level requires a little more risk because it's here that people might disagree. "With all that snow in Minnesota, I sure wouldn't want to live there"; "I think the Braves will make it to the playoffs"; or, "I like the way you fixed your hair this morning." These opinions reveal a little more about who you are and what you believe. Share these ideas with your kids. Look for subjects that might open conversation. Encourage your children to share their opinions as well.

> **TAKE AN INTEREST IN YOUR CHILDREN'S LIVES SIMPLY TO LEARN WHAT'S GOING ON AND GET TO KNOW THEM BETTER.**

Some people are hesitant to share their opinions because they feel like they'll have to back them up or face an argument. Look for ways to affirm your children. "That makes sense" can be an encouraging statement even if you disagree. What you're saying is "I can tell how you came to that conclusion." Or you might say, "That's an interesting perspective," showing that you're genuinely interested in what's going on inside your child.

SOME CHILDREN MAY BE RELUCTANT TO SHARE FEELINGS BECAUSE YOUR FEELINGS MAKE A SIGNIFICANT STATEMENT ABOUT WHO YOU ARE, AND SHARING THEM MAKES YOU VULNERABLE.

Asking questions that don't have a right or wrong answer is often a nonthreatening way to get kids talking. Try questions that draw kids out, such as, "Do you think ...?" and fill in the blank. This could get you off on an interesting journey into your child's heart.

Level 4: Emotions

Facts and opinions often have emotions hidden behind them. "I bet that hurt" or "I can tell you're excited about that" acknowledges feelings your child might be experiencing. Some children may be reluctant to share feelings because your feelings make a significant statement about who you are, and sharing them makes you vulnerable.

Sometimes emotions aren't hidden very well at all. Many kids are quite transparent. "It sounds like that makes you angry" or "I can tell you're disappointed" may be ways to acknowledge those feelings. "I can see why you're angry" or "I'd be disappointed too" may be a way for you to show empathy.

You may need to draw emotions out. "How do you feel about that?" and "Does that bother you?" are good questions to draw the conversation to an emotional level.

If your children have a hard time sharing their emotions, you might start by talking about hope. It's one of the easier emotions for many children to speak about. "What are you hoping will happen in that class?" or "What are your hopes for spring vacation?" Children tend to move more freely into discussions about dreams and imagination, which gives you opportunity to engage them further about how those things would make them feel.

Level 5: Spiritual Closeness

Praying together, sharing what God is teaching you, enjoying worship together, and having a sense of spiritual fellowship are the deepest levels of communication. Sometimes children can't communicate on this level and seem closed when you try. Habits of family devotions and spiritual relationship are good, but they don't guarantee deeper communication if other things dominate the heart.

SERVING OTHERS IS JUST ONE WAY THAT PARENTS AND CHILDREN CAN GROW TOGETHER SPIRITUALLY.

Ask your kids, "How can I pray for you?" They may not have an answer, but pray regularly for them anyway and tell them you're doing so. Ask them to pray for you, too. Look for ways to work together in ministry—providing a meal for a needy family, helping at church together, or visiting a nursing home. Serving others is just one way that parents and children can grow together spiritually.

Attending church, then discussing what you're learning can help foster spiritual closeness. Some families have a regular devotional time together to create spiritual-growth opportunities that don't happen unless they're planned. As you strengthen your spiritual lives together, you'll see more and more opportunities to discuss heart issues.

CHILDREN OFTEN RESIST LOVE WHEN THEY NEED IT THE MOST.

What If I Don't Feel Like It?

Some parents lose their desire to communicate on a deeper level because their children reject their opinions, feelings, or initiative. That hurts. It may take a while for your children to see you're trying to connect in significant ways. You may have to discipline a child for insensitivity or meanness, but continue to explain to your kids what you're doing. Children often resist love when they need it the most.

To help you persevere in difficult relationships where you feel like you're not making progress, consider two passages of Scripture.

Colossians 3:23–24 is directed to slaves, but its application is appropriate for any relationship: "Whatever you do, work at it with all your heart, as working for the Lord, not for men, since you know that you will receive an inheritance from the Lord as a reward. It is the Lord Christ you are serving." When you try to go deeper in a relationship, you may not experience many rewards at first. Keep going, knowing you're doing the right thing and pleasing the Lord. Look to him for approval instead of to the relationship for rewards. That provides inner strength to continue on even after you feel like quitting.

Another passage directed at slaves, 1 Peter 2:20–21, says, "If you suffer for doing good and you endure it, this is commendable before God. To this you were called, because Christ suffered for you, leaving you an example, that you should follow in his steps." In case you think this idea is only for slaves and not for the family, look a few verses later: "Wives, in the same way ..." (3:1) and then farther down, "Husbands, in the same way ..." (3:7). Relating well with others in spite of their unkindness is a way of serving the Lord both inside and outside the family.

Communication in any relationship takes work. It's nice when someone will listen to you and allow you to pour out your thoughts, hopes, and feelings. Listening is a servant task requiring concentrated effort and creativity to get around the barriers and mine fields that can come up. Do the hard work in this area, though, and you'll see positive results.

The Gratefulness Principle

Every person's heart contains a "gratefulness button." Seven-year-old Joshua beams when Mom holds out a plate of cookies and says, "I made your favorites." Mom found the button. Seventeen-year-old Sandra is pleasantly surprised that Mom washed the black pants she wants to wear to the party. Her eyes get big with delight, and Mom knows she's touched her daughter's heart. You feel grateful when your son surprises you by cleaning up the kitchen without being asked, and you give him a big thank-you hug.

IF YOU RECOGNIZE HOW LARGE AN OFFENSE GOD FORGAVE YOU, YOUR GRATEFULNESS WILL ENABLE YOU TO MORE EASILY FORGIVE SOMEONE'S OFFENSE AGAINST YOU.

Gratitude increases closeness. It's useful in parent-child relationships but is also important in marriage, the workplace, and with friends. Romans 12:20–21 even uses the principle of gratefulness to teach people how to treat their enemies. "If your enemy is hungry, feed him; if he is thirsty, give him something to drink. In doing this, you will heap burning coals on his head. Do not be overcome by evil, but overcome evil with good." Paul advised us to treat our enemies kindly in hopes that our actions will trigger their sense of gratefulness and bring the relationship closer.

Matthew 18 uses the gratefulness principle to help people understand how they can forgive others. If you recognize how large an offense God forgave you, your gratefulness will enable you to more easily forgive someone's offense against you.

Look for opportunities to take advantage of gratefulness as you work to draw closer to your kids. Give your children small gifts of love day after day. Be careful, though, that you don't confuse the gratefulness principle with the overindulgence trap. Some parents, wanting their children to like them, recognize giving gifts opens the heart, so they overdo it by giving them too many things. Giving to your kids must be tied into relationship, or the gifts feed selfishness instead of gratefulness.

"My kids aren't grateful. They're demanding, self-centered, and treat me like dirt," said Donna, who sat in our office, frustrated. Her children were twelve, nine, and seven. "My kids only think about themselves and what they want. They expect me to give and give, and they don't appreciate the things I do for them already."

We knew we had some work to do to help this mom before she'd be willing to begin a plan of emotional connectedness. Together we made a list of many of the things she did for her kids. She drove them places, bought them clothes and toys, paid for lessons and classes, attended their activities, met with teachers—and that didn't even count the washing, cooking, cleaning, and repairing required to keep everything running. Donna obviously sacrificed for her children, and she did it willingly with a good attitude. That's why their ungrateful and demanding attitude hurt so much.

When we began discussing the idea of overindulgence, Donna defended herself. "I don't give my kids half of what others in the neighborhood give their kids." That might have been true, but we helped this mom understand overindulgence isn't something you can compare to other families. Overindulgence is simply giving your children more than their character can handle. In fact, when children lack gratitude, the more you give them, the less they appreciate. Although parents love their children and want to give to them, they must restrain themselves or they'll exceed their children's ability to manage the blessings.

> **OVERINDULGED CHILDREN RARELY BECOME GRATEFUL WHEN YOU GIVE THEM MORE THINGS; THEY GROW TO BE MORE SPOILED, DEMANDING, AND SELFISH.**

Overindulged children rarely become grateful when you give them more things; they grow to be more spoiled, demanding, and selfish. Parents then feel unappreciated and become resentful. The hearts of both parents and children harden toward each other, and closeness becomes a thing of the past. When Donna finally arrived in our office, we saw some pretty serious heart issues that had grown over the years in both the kids and their mom.

The solution was to begin with the heart, and emotional connectedness was the window. Donna had already started setting limits in several areas. She learned to make her children wait for things and not always give in to them. Then she began to make small gestures of love to open her children's hearts, looking for signs of appreciation as she went. She gave

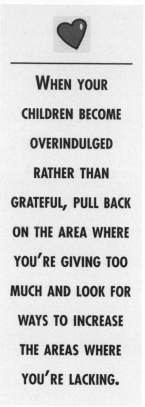

WHEN YOUR CHILDREN BECOME OVERINDULGED RATHER THAN GRATEFUL, PULL BACK ON THE AREA WHERE YOU'RE GIVING TOO MUCH AND LOOK FOR WAYS TO INCREASE THE AREAS WHERE YOU'RE LACKING.

them compliments, encouragement, hugs, and other relational gifts.

Slowly but surely she saw change in her kids. One at a time, these children became more cooperative, helpful, and supportive. After three months of concentrated work on her kids' hearts, Donna told this story: "I can't believe the difference I'm seeing in my children. A couple of months ago, it seemed like our family was falling apart, but now things are much more pleasant. We just got back from a family vacation that went better than I expected. The long drive in the car was peaceful. A few months ago, I dreaded driving even across town. This was a major change in our family."

When your children become overindulged rather than grateful, pull back on the area where you're giving too much and look for ways to increase the areas where you're lacking. Parents rarely overindulge their children in all areas. They usually show love in one favorite way until it's overused and they need to find a different way to push the gratefulness button.

Taylor, for example, gets too many toys and doesn't appreciate them. He may need more parental time and fewer toys. On the other hand, Cara gets lots of "Mommy time." She has become demanding, always needing Mommy to play with her and expecting Mommy to drop everything whenever she calls. Mom may need to set some limits on her instant availability and look for other ways to spark Cara's gratitude.

One dad told us he and his wife had given fourteen-year-old Gracie a cell phone, a computer, a late curfew, lots of clothes, and freedom to choose many of her own activities. We helped these parents see Gracie was making some unwise choices and becoming demanding. They reversed course, restricted much of her freedom, and limited her use of electronic toys and shopping.

Gracie was angry. She believed that these things were rights, not gifts. Over several months, Dad and Mom worked hard to continue relationship while pulling back on her privileges. They knew they were being tough on their daughter, so they looked for ways to love her. They greeted her more often, talked to her more about life, and occasionally gave her a gift. They looked for ways to replace tangible things with relational gifts of respect, conversation, and thoughtfulness to teach Gracie about gratefulness.

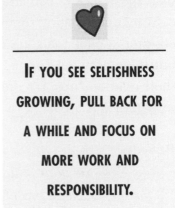

IF YOU SEE SELFISHNESS GROWING, PULL BACK FOR A WHILE AND FOCUS ON MORE WORK AND RESPONSIBILITY.

Teaching the heart gratefulness can be a challenge. Having a child say thank you is just behavior. Gratefulness comes from the heart. Monitor your child's response to gifts of love to determine if you're growing gratitude or overindulgence. As gratefulness increases, you can slowly give blessings in a way that will produce more gratefulness. You'll know if you're moving too quickly by your child's response.

If you see selfishness growing, pull back for a while and focus on more work and responsibility. If the child demonstrates appreciation for your gifts and acts of kindness, move forward. If not, continue to cut back. Some children need years of living on less to appreciate the things they have and the people who helped them get them.

Taking the First Steps

Reaching your child's heart is a long journey and requires you to take the first steps. In this chapter we've given you two ways to start strengthening your heart-level relationship with your child. Many more avenues arrive at the same destination. Your job is to pick one or two to add to what you're already doing. A little work can go a long way.

Time after time, parents describe behavior problems of disrespect, lack of cooperation, or a demanding spirit, and we start by encouraging them to connect emotionally with their children. Other tools are often necessary to teach and train, but the emotional connectedness has the greatest impact on their relationships. It's only a piece of a larger puzzle, but its importance is amazing in the overall parenting process.

Prayer

Lord, as your child I thank you for all you've done for me. Develop gratefulness in my own heart toward you and my family as I try to teach this quality to my children. Help me know how to balance firmness with the gifts of love I want to give. Give me wisdom to know what's best for my child in this area. Thank you for loving me and giving me a family. Amen.

Part 3

Working Out
Heart Change

*May the words of my mouth and the meditation of
my heart be pleasing in your sight, O LORD, my
Rock and my Redeemer.*

PSALM 19:14

A Heart Story
from the Bible

Abram was an old man, ninety-nine years old to be exact. It had been twenty-four years now since God had told him to leave his home and go to the new land. Abram obeyed because he knew obeying was the right thing to do.

Also, there was the covenant. God had made him a promise way back then—so far back it seemed like a dream. *But it's been so long. I must have misunderstood. I thought God said I would be the father of a great nation. Sarai and I don't even have one child. God must have meant something else. Now, twenty-four years later, here I am, no better off than I was back then.*

Although Abram didn't realize it yet, today would be different. The Bible tells us God appeared to Abram. In that special meeting, God changed his name from Abram to Abraham and his wife's name from Sarai to Sarah. God also shared some rather shocking news about Sarah: "I will bless her and will surely give you a son by her. I will bless her so that she will be the mother of nations; kings of peoples will come from her" (Gen. 17:16).

Abraham fell facedown before the Lord. His doubts bothered him as he considered how old he and Sarah were. He began to talk to himself in his heart. *Could it be true? No, that's impossible. She's ninety. She can't have a baby. God must mean something else.* Abraham laughed. *God must be referring to Ishmael, the son of Sarah's handmaid. God must want to do something special through him.*

God knew what Abraham was saying in his heart, and it wasn't helpful. In fact, it was wrong. Without more guidance, Abraham would misunderstand the promise. So God continued. "Sarah will bear you a son, and you will call him Isaac" (Gen. 17:19).

Although it was hard to believe, Abraham now knew what God was planning to do. It seemed crazy, but God had said it. On that very day, Abraham recommitted his life and his family to the Lord. God took the extra time to teach Abraham the truth so that he wouldn't be misled by a lie.

(This story was taken from Genesis 17.)

Chapter 9

Talking to Yourself

The word *heart* is used more than twenty-five times in the Bible in passages where people talk to themselves. The New International Version usually translates these words "talked to himself." The King James Version translates them "said in his heart." For example, when the priest observed Hannah in the temple, he saw that her lips were moving, but she was speaking in her heart (1 Sam. 1:13). Esau was so angry that he said in his heart, "I will kill my brother Jacob" (Gen. 27:41). David wrote in the psalms that the fool says in his heart there is no God (Ps. 14:1).

It's been said that if you talk to yourself you'll be locked up, and if you answer back they'll throw away the key. In reality, we all have inner conversations that help guide us through life situations and improve how we do things. On the one hand you say to yourself, "Here's an idea that may work." Then quickly you answer, "Yes, but if it fails, people will laugh at me." This kind of interaction happens continually throughout every day. Many people do their processing internally, but some people think best while talking out loud. Either way, what we say in our hearts becomes the garden where ideas grow into commitments, and thoughts turn into beliefs.

When people talk to themselves in their hearts, they wrestle with how they'll handle a particular situation. Information is understood in the head, but those lessons are embraced and applied to life in the heart. When they're angry, some children talk themselves into revenge and further anger. Small fears turn into dread when children exaggerate apprehension in their hearts. But when people know how to talk to themselves in helpful ways, they coax themselves through difficult situations calmly and patiently.

CHILDREN'S HEARTS RULE THEIR WORLDS.

Children's hearts rule their worlds. They sometimes repeat false statements or ideas in their hearts that are counterproductive. When they're struggling in relationships, much of what they say to themselves is negative and critical. One transparent twelve-year-old said, "I feel like I have a watchdog in my heart that always looks for things I do wrong."

If you spend time talking to children about their anger, defiance, jealousy, or conflict, you hear some amazing misconceptions about life. Children believe things like the following:

♥ Anger is the best way to solve problems.

♥ It's okay to deceive people if I just lead them on without actually saying something that's not true.

♥ Chores are Mom's job.

♥ Homework is a waste of time.

♥ I was in this family first, so all the toys are mine.

♥ Work should be avoided at all cost.

♥ I can never do anything right.

♥ Mom and Dad shouldn't interrupt me while I'm playing.

When children say these kinds of things to themselves, it's

no wonder their actions end up angry, mean, and rebellious. Ten-year-old Carl had been cutting his skin with a knife, so his mom brought him to us for help. As we talked to Carl, he opened up and shared freely with us. "I hate myself."

"It sounds like you're unhappy with life. If you could change one thing about who you are, what would it be?"

"It's the divorce. I hate it that my parents are getting a divorce."

As we continued to talk with Carl, we discovered he had a number of misconceptions. Some he could only feel, and others he could articulate, such as "Only intact families can be successful," "My life is ruined now," and "I'll have to choose between my mom and my dad."

We helped Carl by teaching him some new truths. His parents had tried to tell him some of these very same things, but he wasn't able to hear the truth from them. We talked about how divorce is terrible, with many negative consequences, but that *his response* to those things was very important. We helped him see that both his parents loved him and he could love them both too.

One line of thinking was especially helpful for Carl. We talked about several people in the Bible who grew up in nontraditional families and how God used them in great ways. Daniel, Esther, Joseph, and Moses each had a story of God's grace in their lives despite their family problems.

Carl liked that. As we continued to talk, we realized this new way of looking at the situation had a freeing effect on him. By looking at the Bible, he was able to unplug his self-concept from his family issues and plug it into God. We helped him develop a greater sense of identity with God as his heavenly Father.

Carl began to say different things in his heart. "God's going to use me even if I have family problems," "God has a special plan for my life and I can talk to him directly," and "God is looking out for me." Carl needed to change what he was saying in his heart. God allowed us to be part of that work.

Kids Struggle in Different Ways

Children of all ages need to learn how to tell themselves the right things, but this idea is especially helpful for teenagers who are in a God-given stage of self-evaluation. Their mission during adolescence is to discover and accept a value system for themselves. Some children struggle with things externally, acting out, getting in trouble at school or with the law, and disobeying their parents. Through these actions they often learn valuable life lessons. It's not the best way to learn, and the experiences they face are often unforgiving and painful.

Other teens may conform to the rules outwardly, but inside they're wrestling just as fervently—and significantly— as the outwardly rebellious child. They mull things over and make wishes and longings. The actions may look different, but the heart-struggle is the same.

SOMETIMES THE CHILD WHO APPEARS TO BE COMPLIANT REQUIRES MORE ATTENTION AND CARE, BECAUSE THE LESSONS HE NEEDS WON'T BE LEARNED FROM AN EXTERNAL CRISIS.

The story of the prodigal son, found in Luke 15:11–32, illustrates this well. The young man ran away from home and wasted a lot of money. He was rebellious in his heart and acted it out by running away. But that wasn't the end of the story. He changed his heart and came back a more humble man. When he came home, Dad was excited to see him. While the focus is on the younger brother in the parable, we get a glimpse into the internal struggles of the older brother as he reacts to the party atmosphere. He, too, had a heart problem. He just dealt with it in different ways.

Some parents spend a lot of energy trying to help the prodigal and not as much on the child who conforms outwardly. Both need help. In fact, sometimes the child who appears to be compliant requires more attention and care, because the lessons he needs won't be learned from an external crisis. The quieter child has internal crises that eventually come out, but they usually take a lot longer to develop. Unfortunately, they're often more serious and require more care to resolve.

The only solution in each case is to help children on a heart level. What are your children saying in their hearts? When you listen, you'll learn where you need to concentrate your time and energy.

Things Kids Say in Their Hearts

As we meet with children about the issues they have with parents, we love to just listen to them talk. It's amazing how transparent children can be when you take time to actively hear what they have to say. After listening for a while, we're often able to identify some key thinking errors that perpetuate the child's problems.

People often jump to conclusions based on limited information. This isn't all bad; it's actually a shortcut that relieves us from the task of continually analyzing every decision. Sometimes, however, when we base conclusions on incomplete data, we end up with wrong decisions. While listening to your children, you can learn more about what misconceptions they may be harboring.

As you learn to listen to your child's heart, identify target areas that you sense are a problem. Behavior indicates what's happening inside, so when you see a particular weakness, jot it down on a piece of paper. You might list things like procrastination, pride, fear, gloom and doom, or lack of confidence. You've probably known these character weaknesses were causing problems. Now you're ready to do some deeper work in your child's heart.

LOOK FOR OPPORTUNITIES TO ASK NONTHREATENING QUESTIONS TO DRAW YOUR CHILD OUT.

Ask yourself some questions about your children. What weaknesses do they have? What lies do they believe? What are some of the unproductive things they're saying in their hearts? Take time to simply make observations and write them down. Ask yourself: What does he say when he's arguing with me? What does she say when she's angry? What does he mumble under his breath in his room or as he stomps down the hall? How does she report offenses to her friends? How does she rationalize and justify her mistakes? As you listen to your child talk, you'll get a bigger picture of beliefs, values, and impressions that are guiding behavior.

Also, look for opportunities to ask nonthreatening questions to draw your child out. This will help you fill out the data you're collecting. Remember, though, that you're looking for information. You don't want to come across as condemning or judgmental. This isn't the time for a lecture. Just ask the questions. "Why do you put off the job of cleaning up that game in the playroom?" or "I'm curious; why do you get frustrated when I tell you to do something?" or "It seems to me that sometimes you're hesitant to try something new; why is that?"

These gentle but probing questions often reveal interesting thought patterns, but it's usually unhelpful to challenge the wrong thinking on the spot. Sometimes it's okay, especially if your child seems responsive, but don't feel like you have to respond just because you hear something wrong. Instead, just give your child the gift of noncritical listening. Then log the ideas and come back later with your observations and comments. Behavior may tell us that there's a problem, but a heart-based solution will take some more detective work.

One six-year-old boy wanted a puppy. Mom listened to him talk and realized he was seeing only part of the issue. He was saying things to himself such as "Puppies are cute"; "Puppies are fun to play with"; "A puppy would keep me company when I'm bored or lonely." Mom was concerned that his perception was unrealistic, so she helped him understand some other facts. "Puppies cry at night, make messes in the house, and chew on shoes and baseball gloves." After considering this new information, her son decided he didn't really want a puppy after all. Mom helped him come to a different conclusion by providing new information to process in his heart.

Of course, just providing information doesn't always get it into the deeper areas where data is applied to life. You may feel like you "share the facts" over and over again, but your child still wants the puppy. This might be because the new information is just head knowledge and hasn't sunk into your child's heart, or the new information isn't sufficient to change the strong desire. Sometimes it takes experience to move facts from our heads into our hearts. Taking care of a borrowed puppy for a weekend may help a child recognize the work involved and provide the basis for a more realistic decision about doing it full time.

As you identify problem areas, continue to interact with

your children and keep a journal of the messages you hear them saying to themselves. A child who procrastinates may be saying things such as "If I leave it alone, someone else will do the job"; "I'll have more time and energy later to do this"; "I just don't feel like doing it, so I'll wait until I do"; or "I'm tired. I've had a hard day. I deserve a break."

As adults, we know procrastination can be a problem because we never feel like doing some jobs, and other jobs won't get done if we don't do them. The mature person says something different in his heart and responds then with different behavior.

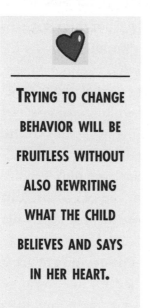

TRYING TO CHANGE BEHAVIOR WILL BE FRUITLESS WITHOUT ALSO REWRITING WHAT THE CHILD BELIEVES AND SAYS IN HER HEART.

A prideful child may say in his heart, "I deserve something you don't deserve because I'm better than you" or "How dare you tell me what to do? Who do you think you are?" This child needs to begin to value servanthood and develop humility.

A child struggling with fear might say, "If I mess up, someone is going to yell at me" or "Better safe than sorry." And a child who struggles with gloom-and-doom thinking usually says things like "No matter what I do, I'll fail; this is hopeless"; "Nothing I do works; I can't win"; or "Nobody is on my side; nobody cares about me." Again, the solution for this child is to develop a new script in her heart so she'll act with more courage and self-confidence. Simply trying to change behavior will be fruitless without also rewriting what the child believes and says in her heart.

One dad said, "I didn't have to ask my five-year-old son

questions. I just read the newspaper in the playroom while he played with his friends and listened to their conversations." A mom said, "My thirteen-year-old son and I talk in the car. It's not hard to get him talking because he's quite opinionated and loves to tell others what he thinks. I can often pick up the thinking errors while we're just having normal conversations."

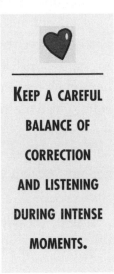

KEEP A CAREFUL BALANCE OF CORRECTION AND LISTENING DURING INTENSE MOMENTS.

Not all children are talkative, and some kids hide what they're thinking from their parents. This makes the task even more difficult. Be on the lookout, though, and recognize they may reveal their hearts at times when you aren't ready to listen. One ten-year-old was hesitant to get out of the car when Mom dropped him off at school. Mom was late for work, so she hurried him along. Afterward, she realized something was going on. That afternoon, she asked her son why he didn't want to get out of the car. He shared a little about a problem he was having with his coach, but she realized she might have learned more if she'd taken the time that morning.

One dad said, "I know that when a person doesn't want to talk, it's frustrating when someone makes him talk anyway, so I want to be careful with my son. I want to know what he's saying to himself, so I probe a little bit at a time. I want to know what he's thinking so I can help guide him if necessary, but I don't want to push him away. I try to draw him out slowly so he doesn't feel like he's being interrogated."

Sometimes children reveal what they're saying in their hearts when they're angry. Instead of listening, parents often react to the disrespect and unkind manner. Children who hurt others when they're angry need correction, but keep in mind that emotion often motivates children to reveal their hearts in ways they might not otherwise. Keep a careful balance of correction and listening during intense moments.

Children also say good things to themselves. Identifying and affirming those statements can perpetuate healthy thinking and positive character development. Bill, age seven, is compassionate, and when someone is hurting he tells himself, "I can help this person feel better." Jim likes to be a leader and says to himself, "If I take charge of this situation, I can make things better." Although both these attitudes could get out of balance in some situations, affirm the good that you see.

Understanding a child's heart isn't easy. But what about parenting is? Proverbs 20:5 says, "The purposes of a man's heart are deep waters, but a man of understanding draws them out." Out of the heart the mouth speaks. (See Matt. 15:18.) Take time to listen. Some messages shout at us; others are subtle. All are significant. Children need our help to correct their thinking errors, so take some time right now and ask God to reveal to you where you need to start.

Prayer

Lord, please teach me to be more transparent with you about the things I'm saying in my heart. I realize you know my heart, and you're eager to help me organize my thoughts around your priorities. Please teach me ways I can help you with the work in my children's hearts. Give me wisdom to know how to guide the way they think about themselves, about life, and especially about you. Amen.

Chapter 10

Teaching Your Child's Heart

Aprimary method God uses to formulate children's hearts is instruction from their parents. Parental teaching gives children the scripts they need as they talk to themselves. Look at how the following verses tie a parent's teaching with a child's heart:

> *My son, keep your father's commands and do not forsake your mother's teaching. Bind them upon your heart forever; fasten them around your neck (Prov. 6:20–21).*

> *My son, do not forget my teaching, but keep my commands in your heart, for they will prolong your life many years and bring you prosperity (Prov. 3:1–2).*

Children develop thinking patterns, paradigms, that determine what they believe, how they will relate to others, what they expect from life, and how they feel in a given situation. These paradigms give children a grid for evaluating life and for making decisions, and they change as a child grows.

Unfortunately, sometimes the conclusions kids come to are naïve or inadequate, creating problems both for the child and often for parents and others. When their grid is faulty, children make poor judgments and react unwisely. As children grow and develop, new information is assimilated into the paradigms, and conclusions are adjusted, sometimes radically.

A TEACHABLE SPIRIT KEEPS A HEART FLEXIBLE, WILLING TO ADJUST TO NEW DATA.

When children are open to new information, they're able to learn a lot in a short period of time. But when a child's paradigms solidify, resistance or even defiance may set in. Parents are often frustrated with their children because they just can't seem to get through—or they see unhealthy or negative patterns that aren't changing.

A teachable spirit keeps a heart flexible, willing to adjust to new data. Parental teaching provides more complete information regularly through instruction, correction, and limit-setting. As children absorb new information about life, their paradigms shift, and those changes contribute to a lifelong growth process.

When parents are intentional about teaching, they can better guide their children's hearts. Much of this teaching takes weeks, months, and even years. As you determine the direction you believe your children need to go, you can modify the way you live, the things you say, and the interactions you have with your child to accomplish your greater goals.

Teaching Happens

Parents are teachers. It's part of the job. In fact, sometimes, we're embarrassed by the things our children pick up at home. One dad told us this story: "My thirteen-year-old son's youth leader came to me with a question a couple weeks ago. She knows me pretty well and knows I have high ethical standards in business. She told me my son was saying, 'What they don't know won't hurt them' to justify taking advantage of another student. When questioned, he said he learned that from the way his dad does his work.

"Apparently my son had heard me talking on the phone to a coworker about a project we were working on. I had said something to the effect that our client didn't understand, and what he didn't know wouldn't hurt him, so go ahead and charge him for it. I wasn't trying to cheat anyone, but I didn't want to take the time to justify the expense. My son took the conversation to mean that if people didn't know, then we could charge them unfairly. This was definitely not my intent. I was surprised to find out he was even listening.

"In the youth meeting, they'd been talking about dishonesty in the story of Ananias and Sapphira. The teacher taught about lying by posing several ethical dilemmas. She was fascinated by the kids' responses and just had to find out more about ours in particular. The situation reminded me I need to be careful what I say in front of my son, because he's watching and learning from me all the time."

Children learn from us more than we realize. They learn how to solve problems, face adversity, and handle life's pressures. Parents teach them how to respond in relationships, show love, and set limits. They learn how to handle emotions, entertain themselves, and respond to disappointment.

Think about the things you learned from your parents. One mom reflected on why she had such a positive attitude in life. "Every night as my dad tucked me in, he'd ask me, 'What was the best part of your day today?' and then he'd say, 'Just wait till tomorrow; it's going to be a great day.' Those nightly comments gave me a hope about life and an excitement about the future that carries me forward even today."

Some parental teaching is intentional because parents decide to communicate information and ideas to their kids.

PARENTS WHO SIMPLY SAY SOMETHING AND EXPECT THEIR CHILDREN TO INSTANTLY CHANGE ARE OFTEN FRUSTRATED.

But many of the things children learn from their parents just happen because they live together or interact with each other. One dad said, "My father was a quiet man and never responded quickly to my requests. It used to frustrate me that he'd take so much time, but now I have kids myself, and I find myself more and more like my dad every day. I see that sometimes I give my kids quick answers to their requests and then I'm sorry later because I didn't have all the facts. Now I take my time, and it's working much better for me. I'm appreciating my father in new ways."

Teaching the Heart

One purpose of parental teaching is molding a child's heart. Teaching isn't just giving information. Integrating facts into life is the goal, and that must go through the heart. Jesus understood this well. He talked about the heart more than forty times in the Gospels. In the Sermon on the Mount alone, he said, "Blessed are the pure in heart" (Matt. 5:8), "Anyone who looks at a woman lustfully has already committed adultery with her in his heart" (v. 28), and "Where your treasure is, there your heart will be also" (6:21).

Children need to believe new truths, value new principles,

and put them all together differently. Parents who simply say something and expect their children to instantly change are often frustrated. They say things like "Why aren't you getting it?" or "How many times do I have to tell you?"

It's one thing to teach children's minds and a completely different thing to teach their hearts. We all know having information in our heads doesn't automatically enable us to apply it. Facts appear in our heads; beliefs appear in our hearts. Beliefs then feed commitments and result in behavior.

Merely giving children facts or telling them what to do does little to impact their hearts. In fact, children can become so accustomed to the rules parents set or the nagging they do, they don't develop the inner motivation to do what's right.

It was Jenn's job to take the dog out for a walk when he barked at the door. Mom would hear the barking and tell Jenn to take the dog out. Jenn would respond, but Mom wanted more. Mom wanted Jenn to see the need herself and do something about it, instead of relying on Mom to tell her. Mom nagged and nagged, but Jenn didn't catch on.

In counseling, we explained to Mom that Jenn lacked the character quality necessary to handle this responsibility on her own. For the purposes of this exercise, we called it "being observant." It turned out Jenn's weakness played out in other areas as well. She'd walk past dirty dishes in the living room and leave her coat on the floor. Jenn needed the character quality of being observant so she could be more effective in life. It wasn't just a problem with the dog, it was a life problem requiring extra teaching and training.

We suggested Mom try something different with Jenn. First, they needed to talk about being observant and how important that quality is for life. Then, instead of telling Jenn the conclusion, "Take the dog out for a walk," Mom was to move back a step. We asked Mom, "How do you know when it's time to take the dog out for a walk?"

"The dog barks."

"That's right, so let's raise the awareness level of that cue."

Mom liked this idea. She explained to Jenn she was stuck in the middle. "When the dog barks, I tell you to take him out. I'd like to see you learn sensitivity here and take initiative on your own. This will help you in other areas of life as well so you don't have to rely on me to tell you what to do. Would you work on being more sensitive to the barking?"

Jenn agreed. Mom still had to coax her daughter for a little while with words like "Jenn, do you hear something?" or "Hmm, the dog is barking," but in the end Jenn made the adjustment herself. She'd learned to rely on Mom to be the cue, and Mom transferred the cue to the dog's bark. Mom had to work herself out of a job to increase her daughter's responsibility. Instead of waiting for Mom to say something, now Jenn is saying different things in her heart. "The dog is barking to go out. That's my job. I need to go take care of it." Or "I better take the dog out before Mom reminds me." Mom was pleased because she knew that these were the very things that responsible people say to themselves. Mom looked for ways to transfer this idea to other areas of Jenn's life as well.

Sometimes parents enjoy being in the middle. They feel needed for a while, but that gets old quickly. When you realize you're caught in the middle, look for ways to help your children connect the dots themselves without your help. It may take some work, because children rely on their parents too much sometimes. It's easy to wait for Mom to set the homework schedule or Dad to decide when it's time to clean the room. But responsibility comes when children talk differently in their hearts. Instead of saying, "I have the right to play this video game all afternoon," they begin to say things like "I better stop playing now because I hear the dog barking" or "It's getting late; I wonder if Mom needs some help with dinner."

Of course some children aren't ready to take these steps of responsibility. For some parents, having a child take initiative sounds like a dream somewhere next to winning the lottery. Keep in mind that children need parental control and leadership to be successful. Hang in there. The child who learns to clean the bedroom every week learns to live in a clean bedroom. Don't be content to just let children fail. Continue to exert parental control until their maturity develops enough to begin the releasing process. Pray that God will do the work of moving the teaching to your child's heart.

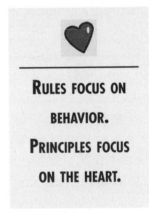

RULES FOCUS ON BEHAVIOR. PRINCIPLES FOCUS ON THE HEART.

When his teenage daughter Katie asked, "What's my curfew this school year?" Fred knew that she was still focusing on rules and likely hadn't embraced any guiding principles of her own in this area. Since college was just around the corner, he decided to take a different approach. "Katie, I want you to come up with a list of principles that helps determine when you might come home. I'm not asking you for a time. I'm asking you for all the reasons why you might stay out late and all the reasons you might come in early. I want to hear what the issues are here—then we'll make a decision together about the time if we need to."

Katie listed a number of reasons for staying out late and coming home early. Fred also explored the disadvantages of each. This discussion gave Katie what she needed to eventually make that kind of decision for herself. Dad still imposed a curfew on his daughter, but the discussion helped him teach Katie principles she'd use both now and in the future. Rules focus on behavior. Principles focus on the heart. When children learn to make decisions for themselves, they're doing the heart work necessary for growing up.

Be deliberate about the lessons your children need, and be ready with creative ideas; communicating beliefs and values takes time and isn't as easy as it sounds.

When Kids Are Wrong

Kids can say some pretty amazing things in their hearts or even out loud. Many parents react to what they hear their children say because they know it's wrong. Sometimes kids'

MANY PARENTS TODAY ARE RIGHT; FEW ARE WISE.

conclusions are not only irritating, they're exasperating. They take parents by surprise, and the shock often causes an explosion on the part of the parent. This reaction then destroys any opportunity to teach. If challenged, a parent may justify a poor response by saying, "But what he was saying was wrong." And of course, the parent is right, but unfortunately, being right isn't good enough. If you want to get to the heart, you also have to be wise. Many parents today are right; few are wise.

One teenage boy said to his mom, "I don't know why I have to mow the lawn. I have to go to school. You don't do anything all day. Why don't you mow the lawn?" As you might imagine, Mom was angry. These were fightin' words. But instead of attacking her son, she walked out of the room.

After thinking about it for a while, she went back and approached her son with sorrow instead of anger. "Son, what you said earlier hurt me. I don't think you realize how much I do for our family. It hurts me that you aren't grateful for those things." Then she left again. A few minutes later, her son came and said, "I'm sorry, Mom. I shouldn't have said that." Mom's approach was successful, and her son learned the things he was saying to himself about his mom were hurtful.

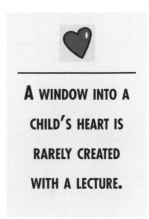

A WINDOW INTO A CHILD'S HEART IS RARELY CREATED WITH A LECTURE.

Look for creative ways to identify thinking errors and reveal truth. A window into a child's heart is rarely created with a lecture. Just because you want to teach doesn't mean your child wants to learn. Teaching is one of the primary windows God has established for parents to reach their kids' hearts, but it takes time and perseverance.

Some Practical Ideas

Once you identify thinking errors, look for creative ways to teach new lessons. Taking extra time to prepare the lesson will make the point hit home more clearly. It's been said that teaching is one quarter preparation and three quarters theater. You can't just figure out what the problem is and react. You must plan well how you're going to address it. Here are a few ideas:

A mom of a six-year-old girl said, "We memorize Bible verses each week in our home. I choose the verses based on needs I see in our family. We've had a number of helpful conversations because of the Scripture we're memorizing."

A mom of a fifteen-year-old boy wrote to us, "We have our son involved in sports and youth group at church. The coach or youth leaders often say things that reinforce the very truths we're teaching at home. Sometimes our kids can hear it better from someone else; then we can just reinforce the lessons."

A dad of a nine-year-old said, "My son and I like to work on my car. We've fixed it up and take it to shows together. The times we're in the garage are great opportunities to talk about things, and my son is usually receptive to my observations about his life."

WHEN YOU DON'T KNOW WHAT YOUR CHILD THINKS ABOUT A PARTICULAR ISSUE, IT MAY BE HELPFUL JUST TO SAY WHAT YOU WISH HE WERE SAYING TO HIMSELF.

Another mom wrote, "My children love books, so I look for those that communicate a message they need to hear. Fiction has a way of grabbing a child's attention and teaching a truth in a subtle but powerful way."

Some parents tell their kids stories about something that happened at work that reveals a lesson. The news often contains stories that illustrate character in one way or another. You might reveal thinking errors by saying, "He thought ..., but what he should have said in his heart was ..."

Of course, everyday correction and instruction provide teachable moments when parents take the extra time to package what they say carefully. Sometimes you'll want to confront a thinking error directly. "You thought ..., but that wasn't helpful. Right thinking in this situation means that you say ..."

When you don't know what your child thinks about a particular issue, it may be helpful just to say what you wish he were saying to himself. You may be challenging his thinking or affirming it. Sometimes it's hard to tell, but either way you're modeling a right heart response.

Children learn how to talk to themselves by the way you talk to them. Model right thinking. Parents often experience the same kinds of problems children face: suffering injustice, dealing with irritation, facing fears, or just doing what has to be done when you don't feel like it. What do you say in your heart in those

DON'T THINK YOU'RE FINISHED JUST BECAUSE YOU MADE SOME WISE STATEMENT TO YOUR CHILD.

moments? You might share your own thoughts with your children so they can hear how to think rightly when they face similar challenges.

Keep in mind that a change in thinking takes time. Don't think you're finished just because you made some wise statement to your child. It's not what you say, it's what your child chooses to believe that becomes his or her reality. Changing what a child says in her heart takes time and repetition. Watch how your kids process the things you teach. When you see changes, affirm them. You might say something like, "I've noticed you're saying new things to yourself about this. Do you see how differently that makes you feel?"

Sometimes children have dreams or ideas you'd like to encourage. Your words envisioning a positive future will become stair steps to help those ideas become reality. Your parenting work is vital; the heart requires training. Children need to learn that if they want to educate their minds, they can go to school—but when it comes to growing their hearts, they need to listen to their parents' teaching.

God Speaks to the Heart

The teaching you do every day has a lasting effect, although you may not see it right away. Sometimes your teaching is planned, other times spontaneous. Sometimes it's easy and sometimes more difficult. Many parents report little progress, then surprising breakthroughs.

YOUR WORK ON THE HEART PAYS HUGE REWARDS.

Five-year-old Titus surprised his dad with this statement: "God spoke to my heart today." Dad loves the Lord and talks with his son often. They memorize Scripture together and pray regularly. "What did he say to you?"

"He told me to honor my mother and my father."

Dad was touched by his son's sensitivity. They had memorized a verse about children honoring parents and talked about what that means. Dad knew he was doing the right thing by talking about the Bible and modeling spirituality with his son. It was a treat to see his son respond on a heart level to what they were learning.

Whether your child responds like Titus or not, your work on the heart pays huge rewards. Look for ways to teach your children, emphasizing practical truths. Watch for teachable moments—often disguised as frustrating experiences—and take advantage of them. You just may find yourself in a great place to do some significant teaching.

Prayer

Lord, I feel like I have so much to learn. It's hard to be a teacher when I'm still in your classroom, but I know I'm just where you want me to be. Please give me the insight I need for my kids. Give me the right words and ideas to share with them that will touch their hearts. I also want to be a responsive student to you. Show me areas of my own heart where I'm saying things that aren't the best. Guide me through the maze, and show me how to deal with my own heart issues in the most productive ways. Amen.

Chapter 11

Meditation Management

Five-year-old Randy's mom asks him to pick up his coat and shoes from the front door. Randy is frustrated because he's playing with his action figures and doesn't like being interrupted. He stomps over to the door and kicks the shoes. Seeing the bad attitude, Mom tells Randy that he needs to sit in the hall for a while. Now Randy is even angrier as he stomps off and plops down in the hall. Mom can hear him from the other room. "I hate those shoes. It's not fair. Mom makes me do all the work. I hate this family. She never makes my brother do anything. I always get in trouble...." And the tirade continues, sometimes loud so that Mom can hear, and sometimes he just mumbles to himself. Either way, Randy is saying these things in his heart. He's churning inside.

Randy is engaged in the process of meditation. We usually think of meditation in a positive way and often associate it with the spiritual discipline of thinking about God and his Word. But meditation also has a negative, counterproductive side: ruminating about revenge, worry, or failure.

Meditation is the process of repeating the same thing over and over again in your heart—sometimes the same words, and other times the same idea examined from various sides.

The focus of the meditation becomes a temporary obsession, and you're not easily distracted from the intense internal dialogue. Sometimes it feels as if your heart is on autopilot and won't stop nagging you about the issue.

Recently a few of our staff were in Chicago's Midway Airport waiting several hours for a flight. Our waiting area was near a moving walkway, and every few seconds we would hear, "The moving walkway is ending. The moving walkway is ending." Over and over the mantra continued, and we laughed at the irritation. It was frustrating to hear the same thing over and over again, but that's what many people do in their hearts. They repeat either helpful or unhelpful things over and over again.

IT'S NOT JUST OUR SPOKEN WORDS THAT CREATE PROBLEMS, BUT INNER WORDS ALSO CAN BUILD SIGNIFICANT ROADBLOCKS IN OUR LIVES.

Randy needs help because the things that churn inside him are self-defeating. He's meditating on his anger. The more he considers the events and his feelings, the more angry he gets. The psalmist wrote, "May the words of my mouth and the meditation of my heart be pleasing in your sight, O LORD, my Rock and my Redeemer" (Ps. 19:14). Notice the Bible says meditation takes place in the heart. It's not just our spoken words that create problems, but inner words also can build significant roadblocks in our lives.

The Power of Meditation

The process of internal deliberation can be helpful because it often enables children to come to decisions and conclusions.

But sometimes those decisions are wrong, requiring correction. Other times, kids just get tired of mulling over the same thing without any resolution, making them more open to an alternative way of looking at their situation.

Krista, twelve years old, worries. She imagines forgetting an assignment and doing poorly on a test in school. She asks her mom question after question. "What if I didn't know a test was coming and I failed it?" "What if the teacher sent home a note to tell everyone, and I didn't get it?" "What will happen if I get a bad grade in this class? What would that do to my average? Would I lose the privilege of being a cafeteria helper?" Krista invests a lot of her time imagining potential disasters resulting from small mistakes in her life. Her meditation gets carried away, going beyond responsibility to living in fear.

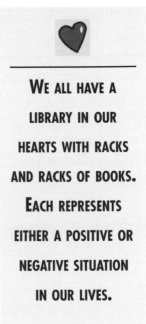

WE ALL HAVE A LIBRARY IN OUR HEARTS WITH RACKS AND RACKS OF BOOKS. EACH REPRESENTS EITHER A POSITIVE OR NEGATIVE SITUATION IN OUR LIVES.

Tommy is angry with his mom because she won't let him go to his friend's house, yet she allows his sister to go play at Jill's. He goes to his room, where his heart churns over the offense for an hour. When he gets tired of meditating on that problem, his heart remembers another offense. Yesterday his mom made him clean his room and miss out on the neighborhood baseball game. Tommy's anger festers for hours as he meditates on the thought that his mom is unfair.

We all have a library in our hearts with racks and racks of books. Each represents either a positive or negative situation in our lives. Tommy chooses to spend time in the anger section of his library. Krista chooses the "what if" section. When they finish considering one book, they put it on the shelf and easily find another in the same area. In fact, children tend to build their libraries selectively. They add books one at a time based on their perception of life and their experiences, and reread them repeatedly in their hearts.

One parenting challenge you face is adjusting the scripts your children play in their heads. The heart churns to try to work things out, but, given some children's beliefs, the churning will never resolve itself. If not checked, unhelpful thinking patterns develop into lifelong challenges.

At sixteen, Vanessa has developed an eating disorder. Although she's thin and attractive, she believes she's fat and ugly. Her continual contemplation of her appearance drives her to unhealthy choices.

Ralph believes he's a failure. He dwells on his mistakes and tends to imagine he's inadequate. When he isn't picked first from a group of twenty students, he believes it's because he's no good. If he doesn't get the best grade on the test, it's because he's stupid. Ralph is headed down a negative path because he's meditating on the wrong books in his library.

Jody blames others and never takes responsibility for a problem. It's always someone else's fault. Jody meditates on all the other factors that went into a problem but won't look at his own part. He's continually unhappy because his perception is that other people make him miserable. He believes that if others would get their acts together, he'd be fine.

Each of these children demonstrates behavior problems due to unresolved heart issues. Your child's problem may not be as extreme as these, but you'll want to look for small errors that can turn into larger ones if not checked. The things children meditate on get stronger. The child who meditates on fear becomes more fearful; the angry child becomes angrier.

When possible, identify unhealthy thinking patterns early and look for ways to counter them.

Changing the Patterns

Children often develop unhelpful meditation patterns and need to change their deeply ingrained habits of thinking.

Joshua 1:8 tells us, "Do not let this Book of the Law depart from your mouth; meditate on it day and night, so that you may be careful to do everything written in it. Then you will be prosperous and successful." Joshua wanted his people to know that the things they meditated on would affect the way they lived. Meditating on God's Word will, of course, bring about right living. Meditation moves thoughts from the head to the heart, where they turn into action.

Changing how children speak to themselves is a challenge. God uses parents to help mold what kids say in their hearts. They also benefit from the influence of coaches, youth leaders, teachers, and other family members. Children with serious meditation problems may need counseling or, in extreme cases, even a residential treatment program to help them change unhealthy patterns.

God also uses events and experiences to change hearts. The apostle Paul experienced a crisis of blindness and a new revelation of who God is. Moses came across a burning bush that God used to attract his attention and then speak to him. We always need to pray that God will do some extraordinary work in our child's life to bring about significant heart change.

ALTHOUGH GOD MAY USE A MIRACLE, HE MORE COMMONLY CHANGES PEOPLE THROUGH GRADUAL, EVERYDAY GROWTH.

Although God may use a miracle, he more commonly changes people through gradual, everyday growth. Heart change is a lifelong experience made up of day-to-day decisions and influences. This is where parents can have a great impact on their children's development.

When you're faced with the difficult challenge of a child whose heart is stubborn and meditating on the wrong things, there are four steps you can use to help bring about change. Making four large-scale changes all at the same time can leave a marked impression. Habits developed over time aren't easy to break, and a multifaceted approach is usually necessary to change a child's heart when meditating on the wrong things has become a lifestyle. The more ingrained the patterns, the more concentrated work is needed. Remember that small changes over time are more realistic than drastic changes.

A WILLINGNESS TO DISCUSS LIFE WITH KIDS IS A GOOD THING, BUT WHEN PARENTS ENCOURAGE DISCUSSION AFTER THEY GIVE THEIR CHILDREN INSTRUCTIONS, CHILDREN MAY DEVELOP THE HABIT OF ARGUING.

1. Remove Old Triggers and Influences

Sometimes familiar life patterns—friends, entertainment choices, or electronics—contribute to unhealthy meditation. Parents may choose to make major changes in their child's life by switching to a different school, encouraging a sport, or cutting out Internet activity for a while. The goal is to change the triggers that lead a child into wrong thinking.

Sometimes, however, the triggers have to do with the family dynamic.

A critical parent can contribute to negative thinking patterns. Allowing siblings to tease unchecked can build a sense of inadequacy. Yelling at kids almost always fosters negative perceptions in their hearts.

Triggers can be hard to see. For example, a willingness to discuss life with kids is a good thing, but when parents encourage discussion after they give their children instructions, children may develop the habit of arguing. Some children even believe that they don't have to obey unless Mom or Dad talks them into it. Inadvertently, these parents encourage negative interaction. Although discussion is good, it's used in the wrong place. Change is necessary for the child to do better.

Limiting a child's freedom, requiring new activities, and cutting back on negative influences can do a lot to change the things kids meditate on and how they perceive life. Removing old triggers and influences helps free children up to develop new ways to think and meditate. It's the first step toward change.

2. Provide a More Structured Life

Children who habitually meditate on the wrong things need a whole new way to live. More structure with less room for going astray can help. Adding structure to common family routines can bring more predictability and accountability to parent-child interactions. Consider changing how you give instructions, for example, and turn old habits into new. You might say to your son, "I've noticed that we do a lot of yelling to each other across the house. From now on, when I give instructions to you I want to be face to face. So sometimes I'm going to come and find out what you're doing first, and other times I'm going to ask you to come to me." Just being close to a child and breaking concentration from an activity can increase cooperation.

When evaluating the instruction process, one dad said, "We decided the job wasn't finished until it was checked. This required each of our children to report back after receiving an instruction and completing the job. This went a long way to help them do the jobs thoroughly and gave us the opportunity to praise them." This dad reported less resistance because expectations were clarified, and his children had better attitudes because the parents intentionally ended the instruction process in a positive way.

TAKE TIME TO EVALUATE YOUR CHILD'S NEEDS AND LOOK FOR EVENTS, ACTIVITIES, AND ENVIRONMENTS THAT ENCOURAGE CONSTRUCTIVE MEDITATION.

Some children have far too much free time on their hands, leaving room for negative patterns. Getting involved in a hobby, sport, class, or activity can motivate children to think about different things. Changing old patterns gives them new things to ponder. Other children may be involved in too much, cramping their schedules and creating a pressure-cooker lifestyle.

Take time to evaluate your child's needs and look for events, activities, and environments that encourage constructive meditation. Remember that each child is different; you may increase the activity in one child's life and decrease it in another's. The goal, though, is the same: to create a structure for your child that works toward healthy internal processing.

Keep in mind that children may resist change. The goal isn't just to make kids happy. Sometimes we must force children out of their comfort zones. Negative patterns are hard to break, and kids often oppose new activities. Things may get worse before they get better. Don't make decisions based solely on your kids' opinions, but look at their lives and determine what changes might improve the conditions that influence their hearts. Then make the changes and live with them for a while.

3. Give More Love

Many wrong thinking patterns children face stem from feelings of not belonging or lack of acceptance. It's logical that a parent's love could combat feelings of inadequacy and lack of motivation, but such emotions as worry and anger also become less intense when children feel loved. Children who experience a lot of love often feel more confident to explore new ways of approaching life.

Joe had a rough time with his daughter, Jeanie. In the middle of her teen years, she spent twelve months in a Teen Challenge program for troubled youth. One of the things she liked was feeling part of the group. "We were all friends, and I loved the other girls in my group. We went through tough times together and learned how to help each other. I just knew they would be there no matter what happened."

Joe saw problems developing in his younger son, Jeremy. Although Jeremy's problems were different from his sister's, Joe decided to put into practice some of the things his family had learned. He began having regular discussions with Jeremy and fostered a deeper relationship through four-wheeling outings. His investment in his son spared him much of the heartache he had experienced with his daughter, and Jeremy's heart made some obvious changes. Joe now credits the extra demonstrations of love as a significant factor in his son's improvement.

Love may simply mean that you connect emotionally with your child, as discussed in earlier chapters, but it's also accomplished by getting children involved in a church or serving on a team. When children feel part of a community, they have a sense of belonging and are more likely to respond positively to adjustments in their thinking patterns. Parents can only go so far to influence their children. Guiding them into other significant relationships offers children love as well.

4. Use the Bible

God's Word can accomplish in a few minutes what might take weeks or months otherwise. Sunday school, youth group, family devotions, and individual reading or study plans are all

THE HEART FEEDS BEHAVIOR, BUT WHAT FEEDS THE HEART?

ways to help children develop healthy meditation patterns. God's Word changes people. We've all listened to a sermon that's had a strong impact on our lives. Bible teachers who explain the Scriptures well help us make life-changing application to our lives. That's heart work. Having children memorize Scripture, hear Bible stories, and discuss Bible passages contributes to positive meditation patterns.

The heart feeds behavior, but what feeds the heart? Children who continually meditate on rebellion and disrespect often display it outwardly. But when children meditate on God's Word, they develop right thinking patterns and a value system that will make them successful in life.

Psalm 1:1–3 tells us, "Blessed is the man who does not walk in the counsel of the wicked or stand in the way of sinners or sit in the seat of mockers. But his delight is in the law of the LORD, and on his law he meditates day and night. He is like a tree planted by streams of water, which yields its fruit in season and whose leaf does not wither. Whatever he does prospers." Meditating on God's Word transforms our hearts.

One dad recalled how learning Bible verses as a child helps him even now. "I remember memorizing Bible passages for prizes at vacation Bible school when I was a kid. They were just words and prizes for me then, but I'm amazed at how much I still remember now as an adult. Sometimes when I'm in a difficult situation or find myself being tempted to do the wrong thing, the Holy Spirit brings those very Bible passages to my mind. Their meaning is clear to me now, and I'm glad I spent the time memorizing them years ago."

Touching the Heart

Teaching kids to think rightly takes time and planning. Understanding what our children meditate on, then looking for ways to correct thinking errors can be one way to touch a child's heart. Look for ways to remove old triggers, create a more structured life, add more love, and use the Bible to do the deeper work.

Prayer

Lord, I'm convicted about the ways I meditate. Sometimes I get sidetracked by focusing too much on certain problems or issues. Please teach me how to maintain a balance of working things out on my own and trusting you to work them out for me. Teach me how to meditate on the right things in my own life. Please give me insight into my children so that I can help them make major changes in the ways they think in their hearts. Amen.

Chapter 12

A Light on the Path to Heart Change

W hile helping children think rightly in their hearts, don't fall into the trap of a simple "positive-thinking" mentality. We aren't just trying to get our kids to "think happy thoughts" so they can fly. That may happen to Peter Pan, but it doesn't happen in real life. Just thinking about your favorite things may get you through a stormy night, as in the movie *The Sound of Music*, but it's often not enough to help children through the deep struggles they face.

Although the Bible's message is positive, it's balanced with a realistic understanding of who we are and what we need. Children need to see the courage of Daniel, who stood for convictions as he faced the lions' den, and hear about Gideon, who was able to fight a huge army with only a few men. Joshua fought the battle of Jericho by trusting God, and David killed a giant with just a few small stones.

The Bible is full of stories of people who succeeded because they trusted God in spite of their own weaknesses. Children find hope, encouragement, and comfort in Bible heroes. They learn about a God who cares about the little guy, about people who can withstand tremendous odds because of their faith, and how God adjusts the natural laws of the universe to help people in need.

One college freshman said, "I can see there are two kinds of people in life: those who take risks and those who don't. Some people, like me, can step out and try new things and aren't afraid to fail. Others have to know all the facts before they're willing to take even the smallest step. I know where I got my ability to take risks. It came from my father, who told me Bible stories all through my childhood. The Old Testament is full of characters who took risks. I always wanted to be like those guys, and when I see someone who is timid, I just want to read the Bible to them. God works in the lives of people who are willing to take risks."

GOD IS BIG, WE'RE SMALL, AND TOGETHER WE CAN FACE A WORLD THAT'S TOUGH.

That young man had it right. The Scriptures give us a clear picture of how God works and put life into proper perspective. The Bible teaches us that God is big, we're small, and together we can face a world that's tough. We all need that message, and children need to see life from God's point of view. It helps them meditate on the right things.

God Is Big

Probably the Bible's most significant message is who God is. Many people don't understand God's awesome power, his divine plan, and his immense love for people. Children can experience God personally and catch a vision for a relationship with him through the Scriptures.

Children need to know that God is creator (Gen. 1:1). He made our world, and just seeing its immensity is startling. It's been suggested that if the earth were the size of the head of a pin, the sun would be the size of a grapefruit eight feet away. The next closest star would be eight thousand miles away. Likewise, each cell in our bodies contains a DNA chain that, if unraveled, would be about six feet long. That DNA contains a blueprint for the uniqueness of each person in the world.

God, in his greatness, has a plan (Eph. 1:11). This plan is so large it encompasses every choice made by every person on our planet. God knows all things. It's fun to ask a six-year-old, "Do you think God understands how a cell phone works?" Many children are surprised to find out that God knows how microwaves work and how computers process information. In fact, recognizing that God not only understands, but is himself foundational to modern technology helps children bring the immensity of God down to a practical level.

It's one thing to recognize that God is Creator and quite another to appreciate the fact that he gave his Son to die for us. John 3:16 summarizes God's plan for the people of this world. It's always a treasure to watch the lightbulbs come on in kids' hearts when they recognize Jesus died for each of them and they can have a special relationship with God.

When children understand the last-days prophecies recorded in the Bible, they see God is also the judge of the world. Someday each of us will appear before his throne. God is bigger than any offense and will judge the righteous and the wicked.

When children understand how big God is, it affects their lives in practical ways. The child who struggles with fear can learn to trust in God. Failure is no longer fatal, but rather an opportunity to ask forgiveness of a God who's capable of removing the sin from our record. Rejection by friends or fellow students is easier to take when you know God created you to be special and he loves you and will never leave you or forsake you. Injustice is easier to let go of because God will judge justly—sometimes immediately, but always in the end. Huge challenges in life are met with the faith demonstrated by Joshua and David. For children, faith isn't something that's merely studied in the classroom. It's worked out in life. And where does the reality of this faith take place? In the heart.

We Are Small

Unlike the positive-thinking movement that says you can do anything, the biblical picture of humanity is that we're sinful, weak, and deeply in need of a Savior. Once that fact is established and personally owned, then we also see how God loves us so much that he picks us out to be special. He has blessed us with every spiritual blessing in Christ (Eph. 1:3).

We're nothing in and of ourselves, but we have everything when we have God living in our lives. Humility isn't inferiority or self-deprecation. Humility is simply recognizing that all that we are and have is because of God's work in our lives. It's okay to admit weakness or to accept failure, because the whole world doesn't revolve around me. We trust in something much bigger than ourselves.

WHEN A CHILD UNDERSTANDS THAT SIGNIFICANCE COMES NOT IN WHO YOU ARE BUT IN WHO YOU KNOW, HE REALIZES HE DOESN'T HAVE ANYTHING TO PROVE.

The Bible teaches children that it's okay to be weak if you're trusting in God. It's okay to only have a little because God turns our little into big things. Some children believe they have to prove to themselves and others that they're significant, worthwhile, and loveable. God's view of greatness doesn't come through accomplishment, talent, intelligence, or good looks. It comes through trust in him. In our weakness, God reveals his strength.

The recognition that weakness is okay is freeing. When a child understands that significance comes not in who you are but in who you know, he realizes he doesn't have anything to prove. God doesn't expect us to reach a level of excellence to receive his love. He gives it to us now. He desires to work in our lives now. The challenge each day is to seek God and his will and serve him. When children get a grip on this concept, they can relate to themselves and others more effectively.

Together We Can Face the World

God's message is one of triumph: "Go out there and do it. Serve me. Take a stand for righteousness. Be wise. Let's go and make a difference in this world. Yes, you'll get bumped and bruised. Don't despair. That's part of life and even part of my ultimate plan. I'll even use struggles and failures in your life to bring about good."

In essence, God says, "I'll be with you, and we'll go on together." You can't lose with God on your side. Or maybe we should say, we can't lose when we're on God's side.

Spirituality isn't just a Sunday-morning experience. Children learn from parents what faith looks like each day as little pressures, irritations, and responsibilities challenge their peace and joy. Spiritual disciplines like reading God's Word, praying, and attending church facilitate our faith and encourage us to grow.

Sometimes the frustrations of family life cause parents to divorce their faith from the daily grind. There's no greater challenge to living spiritually than family life. Your day-to-day

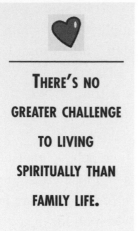

THERE'S NO GREATER CHALLENGE TO LIVING SPIRITUALLY THAN FAMILY LIFE.

integrity is obvious to those who are closest to you. Kids are watching and learning how to apply spiritual truth to life. An apology or an anonymous act of kindness or honesty that costs you something reveals a desire to please God in a humble way.

Although parents may or may not model spirituality, the Bible teaches it in many ways. As you allow God's Word to work in your life and make it available to your children in practical ways, its truths will change the commitments, desires, motivations, and decisions children make. In short, God's Word can change kids' hearts.

Using the Scriptures in Parenting

Hebrews 4:12 says, "For the word of God is living and active. Sharper than any double-edged sword, it penetrates even to dividing soul and spirit, joints and marrow; it judges the thoughts and attitudes of the heart." The Bible is one of the primary tools God uses to change people's hearts.

A careful balance is in order here. Some parents quote Scripture in anger to prove their points or to gain some upper hand in an argument. Although the Bible has tremendous power to work in a child's heart, misuse threatens to weaken its impact. Children who are beaten over the head with the Bible develop a resistance to its message. Guard against that danger and look for ways to capitalize on Scripture's power as you address thinking errors in your children.

Here are some suggestions that will help you get the message of God's Word into your kids' hearts.

1. Study God's Word Yourself

Read the Bible looking for applications for family life. Don't limit yourself to passages that talk about family roles and relationships. Verses such as Ephesians 6:1–4 talk about children obeying and showing honor. They're helpful, but there's much more for families in God's Word.

Elijah was discouraged because he felt like he was alone (1 Kings 19:1–18). Pilate had to choose between peer pressure and what he knew was right (Matt. 27:11–26). Esau had to deal with the hurt caused by his brother, who stole his blessing (Gen. 27:41–42). Each of these stories teaches a valuable lesson to children struggling with similar situations.

Consider taking a year to read through the Bible from a family perspective. Take good notes and create lists of ideas to come back to later. You'll be surprised at the number of Bible passages that will help you and your children deal with family life.

One dad told a story about his eleven-year-old son, Jason, who was treated harshly and unfairly by a teacher at school. Jason felt helpless and angry and asked his dad to intervene and take the teacher to task. Dad chose a different approach because he wanted his son to learn a valuable heart lesson that was even more important than justice. Just that week, Dad had been reading 1 Peter, and he was ready to talk about it when the situation with his son came up. He said, "Jason, 1 Peter 2:20–23 says you are like Jesus." That got his son's attention and gave Dad the opportunity to continue. "Those verses talk about how Jesus suffered unjustly and how he handled it. His solution for a peaceful heart was that he let God be the judge."

Dad had a great conversation about bullies in life— whether they're adults in the classroom or big kids on the playground. He was able to share with his son that we weren't created to carry out justice for the whole world, and even our own sense of personal justice can lead us to a life of anger.

The result is a heart that churns with anger instead of one that enjoys peace.

Jason responded well, and together he and his dad continued to process frustrating school experiences in ways that grew pillars of strength in Jason's heart.

2. Tell Bible Stories

Young children love a good story. The Bible is full of them. Instead of reading fairy tales to your children, consider telling Bible stories in exciting ways. You might even act out the stories as a family. For example, take the story of Jesus raising Lazarus from the dead. All you need is someone to be Jesus and someone to be dead. Have a good time with the story. One family wrapped toilet paper all around the "dead" person to make it more fun. The young daughter said, "I want to be Jesus." Her brother countered, "You can't be Jesus. You're a girl. *I* want to be Jesus." His sister quickly replied, "You can't be Jesus. You don't act right." Mom and Dad enjoyed watching their kids take turns being Jesus and acting out the story of Lazarus. It was a fun way to teach about what it means to be like Jesus.

What Red Sea does God want you to cross in your life? How might you be tempted to do the wrong thing when no one is watching, as Eve did in the garden? What special job do you think God has for you like he had for Moses? Each of these practical questions takes Bible stories and moves them into a child's heart. Sometimes those stories hit their mark early in life, and sometimes they lie dormant for years, blooming into reality over time.

3. Take Your Kids to Church

Whatever you do, don't make the Bible boring. One dad said he has his three-year-old watch boring lectures on TV to try to train him to sit still in church. No way! Don't teach your children that church is dead and something to be tolerated. It's a fun place to learn and grow. Enroll your kids in your church's children's program where they'll be taught the Bible on their level. If the Sunday school needs help, volunteer.

God's church is the vehicle he's chosen to pass on the salvation message to a hurting world. It's also where believers can grow in their faith. Develop the habit of regularly attending—and participating in—church. Teach children that being a part of God's family is a privilege. As your children build relationships with other Christian adults, they'll hear the same kinds of things from them that you're trying to teach at home.

This is important for teens as they develop their own value systems. Don't let young people choose whether they want to go to youth group. Require it. If the youth group is boring, challenge your kids to bring about positive change.

Kids learn important truths about God's Word at church. He often speaks to their hearts while they're there.

4. Memorize Scripture

It's true that memorization only gets the verse into your head, but that's often the first step to getting it into your heart. Psalm 119:11 says, "I have hidden your word in my heart that I might not sin against you." God's Word contains the antidote for much of the venom children say in their hearts. Asking them to memorize verses about the value of correction (Prov. 6:23), the importance of anger control (Eph. 4:26), or avoiding grumbling and complaining (Phil. 2:14) can be the first step to teaching them different things to say in their hearts.

Jill, age thirteen, had a problem with imagining all kinds of bad things that might happen to her. Mom realized Jill was meditating on potential disasters and worrying about things that were unreasonable. Mom observed that Jill loved to watch disaster movies, and they were obviously affecting her more than she realized. Jill's parents put a stop to the intense action movies for a while, but they knew that their daughter needed more food for her heart. They found several Bible passages that would help Jill when she was tempted to meditate on disaster and motivated her to memorize them.

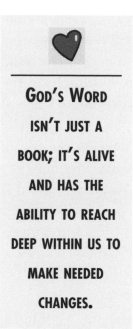

GOD'S WORD ISN'T JUST A BOOK; IT'S ALIVE AND HAS THE ABILITY TO REACH DEEP WITHIN US TO MAKE NEEDED CHANGES.

In particular, Philippians 4:6–8 and Matthew 6:33–34 gave Jill an alternative diet for her heart. It took time, as Jill had to choose to meditate on the right things, but with perseverance God gave her victory over this struggle in her life. Her parents recognized her worry was a heart issue and, as part of their discipline, used Scripture to teach her a new way to meditate.

5. Discuss the Bible

Children of all ages benefit from applying God's Word to their lives. What does it mean in practical terms for a three-year-old to stop complaining? One mom used the picture words in Proverbs 25:11: "A word aptly spoken is like apples of gold in settings of silver." She compared her son's words to different kinds of food, sometimes even pointing to table scraps that are thrown in the trash.

How can a five-year-old apply 1 Timothy 6:18 with his friends as they play together? "Command them to do good, to be rich in good deeds, and to be generous and willing to share." Dad not only asked his son that question, he affirmed him when he did the right thing. "You're obeying the Bible when you share like that, and it makes my heart glad."

Each of these Bible passages gives opportunities for more extensive conversation with children. Teenagers in that God-given stage of adopting their own value systems benefit from discussions about ethical dilemmas, and the Bible becomes a practical guide for choosing those values. For example, how do you know when suffering unjustly is appropriate? After all, God expects believers to take a stand for righteousness. Well, sometimes we need to suffer quietly, and sometimes we need to stand boldly. Older children grow through discussing such biblical issues.

The Bible Changes the Heart

Second Timothy 3:16 tells us that Scripture is "useful for teaching, rebuking, correcting and training in righteousness." Those words summarize much of what we're trying to do in our children's hearts. God's Word isn't just a book; it's alive and has the ability to reach deep within us to make needed changes.

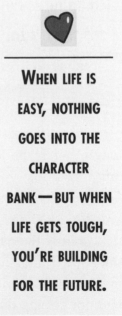

WHEN LIFE IS EASY, NOTHING GOES INTO THE CHARACTER BANK—BUT WHEN LIFE GETS TOUGH, YOU'RE BUILDING FOR THE FUTURE.

Kyle had a general sense of hope-lessness about life. Things were too hard, and he felt that he didn't have what it takes to deal with them. Kyle ended up in our office because his parents knew this was a heart issue and wanted some advice and help with their son.

I (Scott) love to talk to children who've lost hope. The Bible tells them where they can find it. Kids are eager to hear where they can get more hope, because a lack of hope creates discouragement, loss of energy, and a general feeling of gloom and doom. I like to read Romans 5:3–4 and work backward through the verses.

> **OUR JOB IS TO REVEAL THE SCRIPTURES TO OUR KIDS IN WAYS THAT ALLOW THE WORDS TO INCH INTO THEIR HEARTS AND CHANGE HOW THEY TALK TO THEMSELVES AND THEIR VALUES AND BELIEFS.**

"They tell us that character produces hope, but where does character come from? The verse says that character comes from perseverance, but where does that come from? It comes from suffering. Kyle, did you know that when you suffer by choosing to work hard, things start to grow in your heart? The first thing is perseverance. Now perseverance means continuing to do the right thing even after you feel like quitting. It doesn't kick in until you want to quit.

"Think for a moment about cleaning your room when it's very messy. You start to do a little work, and then you feel like this is hopeless and you want to quit. At that moment, perseverance starts. Hang in there, because now you're starting to put character in the bank. When life is easy, nothing goes into the character bank—but when life gets tough, you're building for the future. And, Kyle, here's the amazing thing. After a while of building character through perseverance, hope starts to grow in your heart. Before you know it, it's there and you didn't even realize it."

I met with Kyle for several weeks and enjoyed watching the hope come alive in his heart. He told me how, after learning to work hard, he can now do more than his friends without getting upset. He can hang in there. He's tough and strong. That comes from working hard, learning to persevere, and allowing character to build in the heart. Kyle was learning that hope was actually the reward for hard work.

Where did all this come from? It came from the Bible. God's Word is practical and relates to kids' lives. Our job is to reveal the Scriptures to our kids in ways that allow the words to inch into their hearts and change their values and beliefs and how they talk to themselves. The work you do to understand the Bible and then teach it to your children will have a significant impact, not just for their future, but now in their hearts.

Prayer

Lord, thank you for giving us your Word. Teach me to hide it in my heart like the psalmist said, so I won't sin against you. Use the Bible in my life to teach me how to think rightly, respond to others appropriately, and meditate on the right things. I want to have the mind of Christ, but my thoughts tend to move into counterproductive areas. Please show me through your Word how I can live, not just on the outside, but on the inside as well. Amen.

Part 4

Touching Your Child's Heart

My son, keep your father's commands and do not forsake your mother's teaching. Bind them upon your heart forever ... and the corrections of discipline are the way to life.

PROVERBS 6:20–21, 23

A Heart Story
from the Bible

Hezekiah was very sick. It started with a boil that just got worse and worse. *Will I recover? I've got an idea! I'll call the prophet Isaiah. He'll tell me the truth. After all, I've served the Lord all my life. I don't think God is done with me yet.*

King Hezekiah was one of the few good kings in Judah's history. He was a man of action, reestablishing the priestly duties and getting the temple functioning again. He worked hard to get rid of idolatry in Israel, and he accomplished a lot during his reign of only fourteen years. But he had so much yet to do. He wasn't ready to die.

The officials summoned the prophet Isaiah, who paid a visit to the king. Hezekiah waited as Isaiah sought the Lord. "God says you will not recover. You had better put your house in order. You're going to die."

Hezekiah couldn't believe what he heard. As Isaiah walked out his bedroom door, the king just stared. *Could it be true?* And then Hezekiah began to cry. As the tears came, he turned his face to the wall and prayed, "Lord, I've served you all these years with my whole heart. Please remember how I've walked with you, and heal me. I don't want to die."

A knock on the door interrupted Hezekiah's prayer. "Come in."

It was Isaiah.

"Before I even left your palace, God gave me another message."

"Well, what is it?"

"He told me that he's heard your prayer and seen your tears, and he will heal you. You'll get well in the next three days."

Oh, that is so great. Thank you, Lord. "Isaiah, can you give me a sign that this will actually take place?"

Isaiah thought for a moment. "Yes. In fact, you can choose. See the shadow on the long staircase over there? The sun is setting and the shadow is going down the stairs one at a time. Would you like the shadow to jump ten stairs ahead or ten stairs back?"

"Well, the normal thing is for the sun to go ahead, so I'd like to see the sun go back ten stairs."

"O God of heaven, please reveal yourself to King Hezekiah by moving the shadow back."

Hezekiah's eyes grew wide as he watched! *Whoa! That's really something. I just choose and God does it. That is amazing power.*

During the next three days the king improved. The boil went down. He felt better and could tell he was getting well. He kept thinking about that sign. *I can't believe it. I got to tell God what to do, and he did it.* Pride began to grow in Hezekiah's heart.

A short time later an envoy came to Jerusalem. Guards came to Hezekiah to report the good news. "The king of Babylon heard you were sick and wanted to wish you well, so he sent these messengers."

"Send them in! They can see that I'm well. In fact, I'll take them on a tour of the palace and show them around."

So Hezekiah gave the group from Babylon a personal tour. He showed them room after room of treasures. Hezekiah enjoyed watching their mouths drop open as he opened each door. In fact, the king showed his guests everything, even his armory and all the weapons he'd stored up. Hezekiah didn't realize it, but his pride was getting him further and further into trouble.

"You have done a great job as king. You have so much. Your God must be pleased with you. In fact, we even heard that a miraculous sign happened right here in Jerusalem. Can you tell us about it?"

"Oh yes, you're right. God is pleased with me." Hezekiah smiled. "The sign happened just the other day. I got to tell God what to do. He asked me whether I wanted to have the shadow go back or forward ten steps on that staircase over there. I said 'back,' and that's what he did."

Hezekiah enjoyed telling his guests about all his accomplishments and the miraculous sign. As they were leaving, Isaiah came back into the palace. Hezekiah was about to realize the danger he was in. "Who were those guys?"

"A special envoy from Babylon to wish me well."

"What did you tell them?"

"I showed them all around the palace."

"Oh no. You didn't."

"Yes, I did. Why?"

"You didn't show them all the storehouses and the armory, did you?"

"Yes, but you don't have to worry, Isaiah. They're from hundreds of miles away."

"You are the one who doesn't understand, O King. A time will come when armies from Babylon will conquer Jerusalem and take away all these riches."

At that moment, Hezekiah realized the pride that was in

his heart. *How could I have been so foolish? I was thinking how great I am when I should have been talking about how great God is. I can't believe I did that. I exposed my entire kingdom to danger.*

The king repented. He was sorry for boasting about himself instead of giving God the credit.

Isaiah said, "Because you have responded well to correction, God says he won't allow this judgment to come on Jerusalem during your lifetime."

Hezekiah realized he'd allowed his heart to grow proud. He was grateful for the prophet who corrected him so he could make a change in his heart before he did further damage.

(This story was taken from 2 Chronicles 32:26, 2 Kings 20:1–21, and Isaiah 39:1–8.)

Chapter 13

Constructive Correction

C orrection is one of the tools God uses to touch hearts, and he often uses parents to be like the prophet Isaiah in their kids' lives. But the way you correct your children can mean all the difference between responsiveness and resistance. Correction helps you adjust how children think, feel, and act. When corrected, children may simply change their behavior to conform to parental discipline. When parents correct with an eye on the heart, however, children have an opportunity to readjust their values, rearrange their priorities, and reevaluate their commitments. Those are heart activities.

The Value of Correction Starts with the Parent

Correction helps us change now to avoid bigger problems down the road. "Whoever loves discipline loves knowledge, but he who hates correction is stupid" (Prov. 12:1). "Corrections of discipline are the way to life" (Prov. 6:23). "It is better to heed a wise man's rebuke than to listen to the song of fools" (Eccl. 7:5).

Correction's role is to point out error and redirect a person into more successful ways. With such a noble purpose, one would think correction would be treasured and valued. But several things get in the way, starting right in the heart of the child being corrected.

Children develop the opinion that correction is an attack and they must defend themselves at all costs. They believe correction means weakness, and weakness must be hidden. Angry reactions are perceived as strong. Blaming someone else is considered insightful. Pointing to other factors that caused the problem somehow seems mature. Justifying, rationalizing, and blaming are ways children skirt the issue and miss correction's benefits.

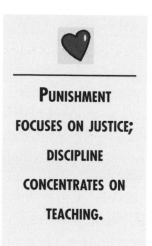

PUNISHMENT FOCUSES ON JUSTICE; DISCIPLINE CONCENTRATES ON TEACHING.

Frustrated parents sometimes contribute to the problem by correcting in counterproductive ways. They may be embarrassed and angry when their children need correction. They seem surprised and caught off guard and end up responding in unhealthy ways. Harshness, criticism, sarcasm, and yelling put children on the defensive. Proverbs 15:1 says that a gentle answer turns away wrath, but a harsh word stirs up anger. When parents act out their frustration during correction they minimize its value.

Parents sometimes misunderstand discipline's goal. They focus on consequences and believe that when they've given the consequence they're done. Punishment focuses on justice; discipline concentrates on teaching. Instead of a sentence to be served, discipline is an opportunity for growth.

One dad told us, "I used to view correction and giving consequences as the same thing. In fact, I had a justice mentality when it came to discipline. My son did this so he deserved that punishment. 'You hurt your brother, so you have to go to your room and play alone.' 'You didn't get your homework done, so you can't go over to your friend's house this evening.' I thought I was correcting my son, but instead I was just acting like a policeman, judge, and jury in his life. I thought my job was just to teach my son that there were consequences for his actions. Now I have a much bigger picture of discipline and correction. My goal is teaching instead of justice. I'm looking for opportunities to help my son grow and mature. Now I seek heart change. I feel like I'm moving my son ahead in life now instead of just putting him down. We're still working on helping him value correction, but my attitude toward the process has helped a lot."

James, age fifteen, said it well: "I want to be successful in life, and I know that other people, including my parents, have some good ideas about what it takes. I try to listen even when someone says something harshly. There's usually something good in their words if I look carefully enough."

Correction is a gift. When children recognize that fact, they'll benefit all their lives. Few enjoy being criticized, constructively or otherwise. The sting of rebuke is seldom pleasant, but its value can be tremendous.

Unfortunately, children don't often appreciate nuggets of parental wisdom. Parents know correction is a gift and are shocked by kids who can't appreciate their sacrifice and care. Sometimes they're offended by the rejection and give up.

THE STING OF REBUKE IS SELDOM PLEASANT, BUT ITS VALUE CAN BE TREMENDOUS.

One mom, exasperated by the continual battle over homework and school assignments, said, "It's not worth it. She can just learn the hard way." Her daughter lacked the motivation to do well and things went downhill at school. Even worse was

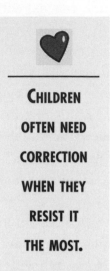

CHILDREN OFTEN NEED CORRECTION WHEN THEY RESIST IT THE MOST.

what was going on inside her daughter's heart. It was clear she even believed she wasn't capable of being a good student. She became more angry at her mom and with life.

Part of your mission is to persevere in correction with your children even when they don't appreciate it. Some children use anger to build a protective wall around themselves to keep others at bay. Your job is to look for ways to penetrate that wall and not be afraid of a child's emotional manipulation. Giving up on the hard work of parenting isn't the answer. Children often need correction when they resist it the most.

Sometimes parents are hesitant to correct their children because they don't want to damage their self-esteem. These parents love their kids and want life to be positive. Some even imagine their child is like a little flower that just needs water and sunshine to grow up to be a beautiful person. These parents are often disappointed when their children aren't as responsive as they had hoped. Anger, selfishness, ingratitude, and meanness leave parents feeling that their child more closely resembles a weed. Some even resign themselves to thinking they just got a bad kid and there isn't much they can do about it.

Instead, children are like a garden where both flowers and weeds grow and where continual weeding and care produce beauty. Left to themselves, children rarely develop the character needed to be successful. Children tend to favor their strengths, and most strengths have inherent weaknesses. Children need complementary character qualities to round out their personalities. Often they can't see what they actually need, so they make foolish mistakes.

Correction is necessary for growth. Imagine if every schoolteacher in America suddenly decided correction was just too painful to administer to students and began marking every answer right. Kids would grow up with a million different answers to questions as fundamental as two plus two, the composition of water, or which side of the road to drive on. Chaos would replace order, and those with right answers would be endangered by those with wrong ones.

It's silly when we think about getting rid of correction—but why then is it so hard to receive? Three things make correction easier to accept: a clear sense of identity, humility, and a vision to grow. Parents may need to step back and work on these three things in their children's lives to develop a greater responsiveness. One of the signs of maturity is the ability to receive correction. It may not happen instantly, but over time children can learn its value.

THREE THINGS MAKE CORRECTION EASIER TO ACCEPT: A CLEAR SENSE OF IDENTITY, HUMILITY, AND A VISION TO GROW.

How Correction Works

We all have a puzzle in our hearts made up of the facts we know, the values we hold, and the commitments we've made. We make assumptions and jump to conclusions about life, and most of the time those leaps make sense and move us in the right direction. We think we've put the puzzle together properly—but sometimes we've jumped to wrong conclusions and made false assumptions. Unfortunately, we can't see the error and proceed anyway, which leads us to erroneous talk or behavior. That's when we need correction. Usually someone who loves us willingly points out the error.

A friend's observation, a bump with reality, or an embarrassing moment may indicate something's wrong in our lives. Our heart has somehow made a mistake and needs adjustment. The wise person accepts the correction and changes. A foolish person continues on, maybe blaming or complaining, until a larger correction makes the error even more obvious.

Children are always learning. They take in new information rapidly and must adjust their hearts regularly. When children hold on to false tenets, they try to force others to adjust. Eventually the truth piles up so much that a child is forced to change and embrace a major truth. Only when that change is made can children make sense of their world and move toward success. Some children, of course, are more stubborn than others, and the process takes longer.

Linda had a problem with her eleven-year-old daughter, Tara. Tara resisted whenever Linda tried to correct her. She typically looked for ways to justify her actions, blame others, or minimize the offense. Linda realized her daughter was saying many unhelpful things to herself when challenged: "Accepting correction means I'm a bad person, so I should try to deflect it somehow"; "I'm justified in doing wrong things because other people are doing wrong things to me"; "Admitting an offense is a sign of weakness"; "I want to be mature, and grown people don't make mistakes, so I must try to appear mature by covering up mistakes."

Mom decided to look for ways to challenge her daughter's erroneous script. She listed the thinking errors and the contrasting right responses, then looked for ways to teach them. When Mom made a mistake, she told her daughter about it and what she did about it, modeling right thinking. She made observations about other people who responded well by saying things such as "Mature people can admit their mistakes and take responsibility for them" and "Correction is good because it helps us change early instead of letting a problem get complicated."

Sometimes Linda was direct with Tara, confronting her for blaming instead of accepting responsibility. Over time, Linda saw the results she was looking for. Change didn't happen quickly, but eventually Tara developed the confidence to accept correction more graciously. Linda was successful with her daughter because she patiently looked for ways to change what Tara said in her heart.

Correcting Wisely

Wise correction keeps kids moving in the right direction, but some parental mistakes can hinder heart change. As we covered earlier, anger, harshness, and intense criticism close a child's heart and make it resistant to change.

"But my kids don't listen unless I get angry." Over and over, we see parents who have bought into this lie. They feel like they have no other choice because of their kids' resistance. After all, anger works. It gets kids moving when chores have to get done. It gets them to stop when they're being annoying. Because it seems to work more quickly than other methods, parents tend to use anger more often.

Unfortunately, anger has many negative side effects, and the biggest is a

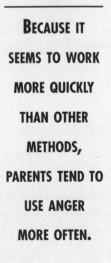

BECAUSE IT SEEMS TO WORK MORE QUICKLY THAN OTHER METHODS, PARENTS TEND TO USE ANGER MORE OFTEN.

decaying relationship. Life isn't just about getting jobs done or stopping children from being annoying. Life is about relationships. Anger only brings about behavior change; it has a limited ability to change a child's heart.

Parents who correct with an eye on the heart do things differently. Here are a few suggestions to get you started.

1. *Focus on teaching instead of justice.* What do you want your child to learn from this experience? Sometimes asking yourself why you're frustrated can get you more focused on the heart than on behavior.

2. *Use sorrow instead of anger.* Sorrow opens doors in relationships; anger builds walls. If you ponder the problem, you'll see that you truly feel sorrow, although your anger may mask it. Communicating sorrow instead of anger can go a long way to touch a child's heart.

3. *Prepare for discipline times by planning consequences.* Don't feel obligated to give a consequence on the spot. Taking some extra time will let you settle down, think, and come up with a productive discipline strategy. Look for ways to tie consequences clearly to life, so children can more easily learn from them.

4. *Talk about character, not just behavior.* When you talk to your child about the problem and about what you'd like to see instead, focus on your child's character strengths and weaknesses, not just the outward actions.

Instilling the Vision

It's not easy for most children—and many adults—to grasp the value of correction. Resistance seems right under the surface, and you feel like you must approach certain subjects gingerly. So look for creative ways to communicate.

One mom taped a three-foot piece of toilet paper to the back of her collar and waited for her children to see it. Her nine-year-old commented first. "Mom, why is that toilet paper on your back?"

Mom immediately acted defensively. "There's no toilet paper on my back," she said angrily.

The twelve-year-old joined the discussion. "Yes there is, Mom. It's a long piece hanging down."

"No there isn't," Mom continued. "Other people always try to make fun of me. You just make things up. You're just trying to make me feel silly."

The two children, seeing Mom acting strangely, got a little more excited and tried to come toward Mom to show her her error.

"Get back. You're always trying to point out something wrong. You don't look at the nice clothes I have on. You're always looking for something bad about me."

The girls were giggling now, knowing Mom was up to something, and they moved closer to try to pull the toilet paper off.

Mom ran away, adding dramatics and wailing. "Just leave me alone. Stop picking on me. You make it sound like I never do anything right. If you would just leave me alone, I would be much happier."

The girls finally grabbed the toilet paper and showed it to their mother.

"*You* must have put that there," Mom said.

The girls laughed, knowing Mom was having fun with them.

After laughing with them, Mom said, "I'm just teasing you, but I wanted to show you that correction is a good thing. Sometimes people whine and complain and ignore it when someone is trying to help them, but correction helps us see things that are out of place in our lives. If we continue without it, we may go on thinking everything is okay when it really isn't."

One dad set up a race through a challenge course for his children ages seven, ten, thirteen, and fifteen. The goal was to cross the playroom without bumping into one of the chairs or stepping on a plate. The children worked in teams with the competitor blindfolded and the partner acting as a coach. After the blindfolds went on, the chairs and plates were rearranged. The coaches guided their siblings through the maze. At first, the two older children wanted to compete, but then they realized their team would do better if they were the coaches.

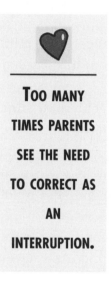

TOO MANY TIMES PARENTS SEE THE NEED TO CORRECT AS AN INTERRUPTION.

When they were done, Dad asked several questions: Why did you older kids want to be the coach instead of the competitor? What does the competitor have to do to win? How does the coach feel when the competitor doesn't seem to be following instructions? Then Dad applied this to his own relationship with them. He was trying to be their coach. Sometimes he might not use the best approach, and he was looking for better ways to correct and redirect them. At the same time, they'd be more successful life competitors if they'd listen to the coach.

What's Your Vision?

Parents, too, must have a vision for correction to guide children through the emotional pitfalls of family life. Too many times parents see the need to correct as an interruption. In reality, children learn character through correction, especially if parents handle it without emotional intensity. It takes many corrections to teach one lesson, but that's part of the parental job description.

Take time right now to evaluate your own feelings about correction. How do you respond when corrected? Consider the role of correction in your life as well as your child's. Once you recognize its importance, you'll be ready next time an opportunity comes. You'll be able to avoid reactive discipline and become more proactive.

Good correction is an art. It's been said that wisdom is being able to give someone a shot in the arm without having him feel the needle. You may think that's impossible as you look at your son or daughter reacting at the smallest inkling of correction. Look for ways to get around their defensiveness. You'll be surprised at how a little work can go a long way.

Be careful to set reasonable expectations for each discipline episode. You're unlikely to see instant change, so correct with an eye on the future, recognizing that change takes time. Just because your child wants to argue doesn't mean you have to join in; sometimes your comment is all that's needed. You've made your point. Let life drive it home.

Parents are both spectators and participants with a vested interest in the outcome of their children's lives. It's hard to watch them go down a difficult path when you know correction will bring them back.

Spend a lot of time praying for your kids. Remember that correction is also part of God's job description, and he's interested in your children too. Model humility during correction, continue to correct even in the face of resistance, look for creative ways to get your point across, and trust God to maximize your work and provide other means to grow your children.

Prayer

Lord, please give me the humility to correct my mistakes. Give me a positive view of correction in

*my own life. Help me to listen to and evaluate oth-
ers' corrective observations and comments. And
Lord, please help me to find ways to correct my children that will produce results. Give me an attitude
about correction that gives my kids a vision to
receive it. Thank you that you love me enough to
correct me. Amen.*

Chapter 14

Turn Around for a Change

Parents sometimes feel like they're correcting their children for the same things over and over. They get frustrated because they just aren't seeing any change. Jack has a temper tantrum every time his mom tries to correct him. Raphael hits his brother when he doesn't get his way. Candace lies to get out of trouble. Parents want the best for their kids, but their children seem bent on doing the wrong thing, and nothing in the discipline department seems to work.

Heart change is key to significant growth, but what does it mean to change one's heart? In this chapter, we'll take apart the change process so you know which pieces you need to concentrate on with your child. Jack, Raphael, and Candace all can change.

A change of heart is complicated, so we've broken it down into six parts, each contributing significantly to growth. Some children need help understanding the process in smaller pieces to be successful. Asking a child to change his heart can be like asking a ten-year-old to clean the house. He'll likely need help knowing what needs to happen first.

Sometimes it's hard to know whether the child's lack of change comes from defiance or just immaturity. By breaking down the process, even young children can learn the individual pieces. Once you know the steps, you can target your correction more specifically, resulting in progress.

The Bible uses the term *repentance* to describe a change of heart. The word *repent* is used more than seventy-five times in the Bible. Looking at these passages gives us a clearer understanding of what repentance means and helps us know how to apply this theological concept to our children.

Although children may not understand how their heart works and may not realize the significance of what they're doing, children do repent. Your success in changing behavior is directly related to their willingness to change their hearts. The Bible places heavy emphasis on personal responsibility in repentance. Each person has the ability to respond properly, and God calls people to repentance regularly.

MANY CHILDREN KEEP THEIR PARENTS AT BAY WITH EXPLOSIVE OUTBURSTS AND MEANNESS. PARENTS EITHER COWER AT A CHILD'S ANGER OR ENGAGE IN AN ESCALATING BATTLE OF INTENSITY. NEITHER HELPS A CHILD CHANGE THE HEART.

It's important, however, to recognize that God is deeply involved in the heart-change process. It's his work of salvation and the continual work of the Holy Spirit that brings lasting change in lives. As you delve into the challenge of working with your child's heart, look for ways to partner with God. Pray for your children often. Ask God to do the deeper work in your child's life and to use you in the process.

Repentance requires the following six steps:

1. Settle Down and Stop Fighting

Realistically, this may be the only step you can require of a child through the correction process. Many children keep their parents at bay with explosive outbursts and meanness. Parents either cower at a child's anger or engage in an escalating battle of intensity. Neither helps a child change the heart.

Mary, a mother of a four-year-old, told us, "My son verbally attacks me whenever I correct him. Before I realize it, I find myself yelling. Somehow the problem then shifts from his issue to our interaction. I can't seem to get anywhere." Mary has it right. By responding to her son's taunts, she accepts the bait her son throws out, and he successfully maneuvers the focus from his own heart to the frustrations of their relationship.

Instead of engaging in a battle with her son, Mary would be much more successful if she refused to get drawn in. She has to stop the process from escalating and require her son to settle down before he's free to do anything else, including having a conversation about the problem.

Jeremiah 8:6 describes an unrepentant person as "a horse charging into battle." You can imagine the nostrils flaring and the eyes widened as the horse rushes ahead. That's an apt description of many unrepentant children bent on doing the wrong thing. The first step in the change process is to settle down and be willing to work on the problem.

Another child's temper tantrum motivates her to follow her mom around the house, making accusations and taunting her. Mom must remain calm and refuse to allow her daughter to draw her into the fight. Trying to go to other steps in the correction process without accomplishing this one usually causes more conflict. Whatever you do, don't make the problem worse by engaging in a battle with your kids.

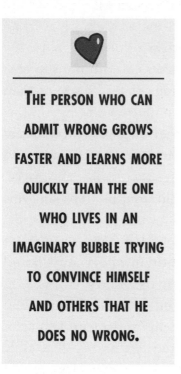

THE PERSON WHO CAN ADMIT WRONG GROWS FASTER AND LEARNS MORE QUICKLY THAN THE ONE WHO LIVES IN AN IMAGINARY BUBBLE TRYING TO CONVINCE HIMSELF AND OTHERS THAT HE DOES NO WRONG.

When Christopher doesn't get what he wants, he runs to his room crying, "You don't love me." His drama tugs at his mother's heart because she doesn't like to see him so sad. However, Christopher too needs to settle down before he and his mom can talk. Concentrate on a plan for settling down. You may need to step into the process earlier by seeing the warning signs at a level three, for example, before your child flies out of control at level ten. Preemptive action can go a long way to keep the intensity down.

Because this step is so important in the correction process, and because many children have a hard time right here, we've devoted the whole next chapter to specific ways to help children settle down. This step is not optional. If you don't work hard on it, you won't get too far toward repentance.

2. Be Willing to Admit You've Done Something Wrong

An essential part of change is admitting you have a problem. First Kings 8:47 describes the repentant person as saying, "We have sinned, we have done wrong, we have acted wickedly." Sometimes children resist change partly because they're telling themselves the lie, "If I admit I'm wrong, then I'm weak." Actually, the person who can admit wrong grows faster and learns more quickly than the one who lives in an imaginary bubble trying to convince himself and others that he does no wrong. Sometimes a child's commitment to self-protection prevents him from growing out of childish choices and responses.

A child may say, "I didn't do anything wrong." Children often don't realize what behaviors contribute to conflict. It's not necessarily wrong to talk about a problem, for example, but when these statements cross the line they can become complaining or arguing. Sometimes "wrong" doesn't require moral implications; it simply means my present behavior isn't working in this situation. Continuing to justify things that don't work keeps a person in a cycle of failure.

As you correct your children, you're responding to their mistakes, blind spots, or wrong actions, but correcting a child once for something may only be the beginning. The child may need multiple observations and even several people to point out the same thing before she's willing to consider the possibility that something's wrong. It's been said that if one person says you have a tail, you can ignore it, but if five people point out your tail, you better turn around and look.

3. Realize There's Something Different You Could Have Done

Most parents, at one time or another, have had the "can't or won't" discussion. Bobby says, "I can't apologize to my teacher," and Mom asks, "You can't or you won't?" Children's unwillingness often stops them from moving forward. Sometimes they continue doing the wrong thing because they don't know another alternative exists. Much of parenting is training our children to think, act, and speak in new ways. The goal of our work is to help children see there is a better way.

IT'S NOT ENOUGH TO PONDER THINGS, EXPERIENCE EMOTIONS, PLAN STRATEGIES, AND EXPLORE ALTERNATIVES. COMMITTING TO A NEW COURSE OF ACTION IS AN ESSENTIAL PART OF REPENTANCE.

People often come to parenting seminars because what they're currently doing isn't working, and they're hungry for new approaches to child training. The things they've done aren't necessarily bad; they just aren't working. The heart-based approach described in this book is significantly different from what many parents are doing. When the lightbulbs come on and parents see this approach makes sense, they're more willing to leave old patterns behind and develop new techniques and strategies.

Children, too, benefit from exploring alternatives to their present ways of reacting or doing things. Sometimes parents correct children by emphasizing the negative: "Stop having a bad attitude" or "Stop fighting with your brother." But here's the important question: What do we want our children to do instead? You may need to camp out on this step and help your child catch a vision for new ways of relating to life.

The child who's often in conflict with others needs to learn new ways of expressing his opinion. The daughter who left her homework undone because it was too hard needs to know she can get help by asking a parent or her teacher. Children who are easily frustrated need to understand what perseverance looks like in practical terms. This step may involve some brainstorming for you and your kids.

4. Commit to Doing the Right Thing

A change of heart is more than just admitting what was wrong and identifying right things to do instead. Repentance means committing to *do* the right thing. In Jeremiah 34:15 God said to the people, "Recently you repented and did what is right in my sight." Commitments are made in the heart. It's not enough to ponder things, experience emotions, plan strategies, and explore alternatives. Committing to a new course of action is an essential part of repentance.

Repentance is often described as a 180-degree turn. You're going one way, recognize the error, and turn completely around and go the other way. That's a good picture because it shows taking steps in a new direction.

To accomplish this goal, some parents have their children role-play a right response to the problem before the discipline time is over. "Jeremy, before you're free to play, you need to show me a good response to my instructions, so I'm going to ask you to do a job right now to see if you can respond in the right way like we talked about." These kinds of reenactments help children envision and anticipate the right thing to do.

New commitments are hard to develop into habits. How many times have you decided to do something differently, only to find the process of change more difficult than you expected? Change often takes practice. You may ask your child to demonstrate the right activity a few times a day to help establish a new pattern. "Debbie, when I call your name, I want you to come to me. Because you've been having trouble with this, we're going to practice. Several times today, I'm going to call your name to see if you can come right away."

Practice times often help children solidify new patterns and develop a commitment to respond differently.

5. Feel Sorrow for Doing the Wrong Thing

The next two repentance steps are difficult to force because they involve emotion and desire. You may not focus on these steps directly, but instead pray that God does this deeper work. Other times, you'll see sorrow in your child and want to encourage it. Ultimately, these steps add significant depth to a change of heart.

Second Corinthians 7:10 says, "Godly sorrow brings repentance." Jeremiah 31:19 says, "After I strayed, I repented; after I came to understand, I beat my breast. I was ashamed and humiliated because I bore the disgrace of my youth."

When a child responds well to correction, you can see sadness for doing the wrong thing. Some children seem to express sorrow naturally. All you have to do is give that look, and your child says, "I'm sorry, Mommy" and changes. Or, when you give a consequence, you can tell the crying isn't vengeful or angry but the repentant cry of a child who recognizes she's done the wrong thing.

The rest of us don't have it so easy. In fact, if your children responded well to correction, you probably wouldn't be reading this book. Most parents just dream of quick and easy heart change. Instead, we live in what some consider a nightmare of continual correction and confrontation. Out of exasperation, many parents look for bigger consequences, thinking something huge will do the trick, but bigger consequences rarely produce long-term change. Small, consistent heart challenges are more likely to do the deeper, lasting work.

Parents intuitively know that repentance involves sorrow. That's often why they require a child to say, "I'm sorry" after an offense. Unfortunately, you can't force emotions. In fact, we'd recommend you not require an "I'm sorry" unless the child is truly feeling sorrow. Instead, have the child say, "I was wrong; will you forgive me?" This is often a more realistic solution for a child who needs to make something right.

Sometimes children have to live with the pain of their choices for a while to feel sorry for a particular problem they've created. The child who gets into debt may take several months to get out and during that time feel frustrated because he can't buy other things. This child may need several weeks of living under financial pressure to feel sorry about getting into that predicament.

> WE'D RECOMMEND YOU NOT REQUIRE AN "I'M SORRY" UNLESS THE CHILD IS TRULY FEELING SORROW. INSTEAD, HAVE THE CHILD SAY, "I WAS WRONG; WILL YOU FORGIVE ME?"

Be on the lookout for examples of sorrow in your child. Encourage it as a sign of maturity and an important part of the change process.

6. Desire to Do the Right Thing

Desiring to do what's right doesn't guarantee someone will actually do it, but desire is a heart activity and another important part of repentance. Paul wrestled with his own desires in Romans 7 when he wrote, "What I want to do I do not do, but what I hate I do" (v. 15). Even children who want to do what's right struggle. As parents, we need to look for ways to help children be more successful at doing the right thing. The desire is there, but the child lacks character or has competing desires that get in the way.

When helping children who are frustrated with themselves because they aren't changing as fast as they'd like, I tell them the story of my (Scott's) baseball career. I played first base for our church softball team. I liked first base because I was in on many plays. I'd get the guy out and then throw the ball back to the pitcher.

The coach came to me one day and said, "When you get someone out and no one else is on base, throw the ball to the other infielders." I liked that idea. I'd even seen professional ball players do that. I decided to change. Unfortunately, my next opportunity didn't come for several plays. When it finally did, I went right back to my old habit and threw the ball back to the pitcher.

"Throw it around," the coach yelled.

"Oh yeah. Sorry, Coach." I made a mental note, but the next time didn't come right away, and when it did, I threw the ball back to the pitcher. But this time, I remembered right away and said, "Oops. I'll do it next time." I recall the next opportunity well. I got the guy out and began to throw the ball back to the pitcher. In midthrow I stopped, turned, and threw the ball to another player. I had made the change. That doesn't mean I never forgot again, but I had successfully brought my actions in line with my desire.

Take a moment to choose a challenging problem you experience with your child. Go through the above steps of repentance and ask yourself, "Where is my child getting stuck?" Then look for strategies to teach, train, and correct in that one area of heart change. Your new, targeted approach will yield small steps of change. Encourage those glimmers of hope, and develop new approaches to make lasting changes in your child's life.

Prayer

Lord, I see areas in my own life that need work. Please show me what changes I need to make in my own heart so I can grow. Give me patient persistence with my kids as I look for ways to motivate them to change their hearts. When I get frustrated with my children, please help me to break down the problem and see specific things I can do to work along with you in their hearts. Amen.

Chapter 15

Defibrillating Your Child's Heart

Perhaps you've watched a TV medical drama in which emergency department doctors hover over a patient, working furiously to save a life. Suddenly one calls for a defibrillator, places the paddles on the patient's chest, and yells, "All clear!" You see the body on the gurney jump, and all eyes turn to the heart monitor. If a regular heartbeat isn't restored, the doctor places the paddles back on the chest, and again we hear, "All clear!" The process is repeated as many times as necessary for the heartbeat and pulse to synchronize so the patient can live.

Likewise, children can become quite stubborn when it comes to evaluating and adjusting their spiritual hearts. Parents then become frustrated, upping the consequences, increasing the yelling, or sometimes giving up the battle. At these moments, a parent's character is tested greatly. But when parents catch a vision for a heart-based approach to correction, they make significant adjustments in their own hearts and develop more courage, patience, perseverance, and love than they ever thought possible. They act as "defibrillators," helping their children regulate the function of the heart and bring it back to a place of growth and development.

Of course, if the greater courage heightens a parent's volume level or adds cynicism and sarcasm to the interaction, heart change in the child is less likely. Instead, parents must stop the skirmishes and change the battlefield from the parent-child relationship to the child's heart.

When children seem bent on doing the wrong thing, parents generally experience two emotions: anger and fear. Life can be unforgiving at times, and the consequences of foolishness can be huge. Children with serious heart issues are in danger. Whether it's the four-year-old who won't come when called, the eight-year-old who's mean, or the fourteen-year-old who's sneaking out of the house, the red warning lights are flashing in Mom's and Dad's minds. Parents are often surprised that their son or daughter would do things that any mature adult knows are self-defeating. You know that if this behavior continues, bigger problems are right around the corner. Kids can't see very far ahead, but you can.

CHILDREN WITH SERIOUS HEART ISSUES ARE IN DANGER.

So what do you do about it? How can you help your children see they're on the wrong path and headed toward failure? God gave correction as a tool to break the negative cycles you see in your child. But where do you start?

Identifying Entry Points

Many parents feel as though their children's hearts are a spinning merry-go-round; they want to jump on and do some work, but the ride is moving too fast, and getting on seems impossible.

Before you give up, take time to evaluate your entry points. Typically, when do you begin correcting a specific problem? Often parents wait until the report card comes or someone gets hurt or the volume level is deafening. Correcting earlier in the process is often more productive and, although resistance is still likely, early intervention is more successful at bringing about heart change.

This requires the parent to identify the child's initial error—the very first comment, action, look, or indication that a problem is on its way. Michele told us, "My twins are always fighting. I think the initial offense was in the womb." Most problems are like that. They have a history, but each episode usually contains a trigger, cue, or initial offense. If you want to find a successful entry point, go back further than you usually do and catch the problem earlier.

Michele had tried several things to get her children to stop the teasing, put-downs, and meanness, with little or no success. Well-meaning friends told her that boys will be boys and that putting up with bickering was part of her job.

After attending one of our seminars, she was eager to try a heart-based approach to address the problem. She examined her interaction with her boys more carefully and realized her correction point was usually later than was helpful. "I disciplined them when things got out of hand, when one was hitting the other, or mean words had escalated into yelling and name-calling. I've done several things differently now. I look for smaller offenses earlier in the process. I also discipline the boys separately instead of together. And I have at least one of them take a Break [see next section and our book *Home Improvement* for a more detailed explanation] and then come back to me for a debriefing. Sometimes I discipline them both, but not always. I've been watching their interaction more closely, and I can actually see the heart problems coming on before they do. That's my cue to take action. I can't believe the difference

I'm seeing. We've got a long way to go, but now I have the tools to get there."

Using a Break

Correcting earlier in the process isn't the whole solution, but it's the first step. Some children lose control quite quickly, however, so parents need tools to bring them back to a place where they can work on the problem. When you see a child going down the wrong path, you might provide a warning. It's always best to start correction with words in hopes that children will respond. Some children will.

MANY PARENTS MAKE THE MISTAKE OF GIVING SEVERAL WARNINGS, THEN EXPLODING WITH FRUSTRATION.

Don't overuse warnings, however. Many parents make the mistake of giving several warnings, then exploding with frustration. If a warning doesn't work, we suggest you move quickly to a Break. The Break is an excellent tool for heart change in children and can be used with toddlers through teenagers. It's actually an adult skill that kids can learn even when they're young.

A Break works wonders in a child's heart because it forces her to stop and ponder the problem rather than continue blaming the problem on others and avoiding personal responsibility. It's not a punishment; it's a heart-adjustment tool.

Children rarely stop to consider their direction. Many are busy and distracted by such things as TV and movies, video games, computers, music, and social relationships. These things aren't necessarily bad, but they can have a hypnotizing effect on children who tend not to consider their ways. Psalm 119:59 says, "I have considered my ways and have turned my steps to your statutes." It's hard to make significant change in life without self-reflection. The Break gives children much-needed opportunities to consider their emotions, values, motivations, commitments, and other heart-related issues.

It's hard to make significant change in life without self-reflection.

The child must go to a Break, settle down, and then return to the parent for a debriefing. For preschool children this place may be right in the same room—on the floor, by the couch, or in front of the refrigerator. For older children, this place may be the stairway or hall. A child's bedroom is a possibility, but kids usually feel relaxed and comfortable in their rooms and are often distracted by toys. Instead, we'd recommend a place that's a little less comfortable, one that gives your child more motivation to do the heart work necessary for change.

Children of all ages benefit from learning to take a Break, but what each child can accomplish varies. Young children may only be able to settle down in the Break; then parents can help them process what's going on. Older children may be able to proceed further through the repentance process. Either way, the Break sets the stage for heart change to begin.

But You Don't Know My Child

Some parents try a Break with their kids and are surprised by the resistance. Don't be deterred if your child is unwilling to go to a Break. Sometimes parents give up because their children resist, but resistance is often just confirmation that they need it. Stubbornness hinders significant change in anyone's life.

Children respond in different ways as they're learning to

take a Break. Some yell and scream while sitting in the Break. Others defiantly put their bottoms down a couple of feet from the place you chose. Some refuse to go, defiantly rejecting the whole process. Hang in there. The Break is essential, and the more you recognize its value, the more you'll want to persevere to make it work in your family.

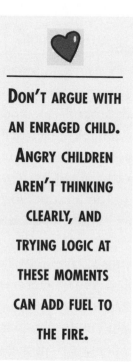

DON'T ARGUE WITH AN ENRAGED CHILD. ANGRY CHILDREN AREN'T THINKING CLEARLY, AND TRYING LOGIC AT THESE MOMENTS CAN ADD FUEL TO THE FIRE.

Some children go to the Break with defiance, anger, and even revenge. "I hate you. Billy always gets me in trouble. You don't understand me." These kinds of statements indicate heart work is taking place, even if it's not moving in the right direction yet, because the heart is where we wrestle with things. Sometimes children wrestle by saying unkind words and building up emotion. If parents address the issues properly, they can help children turn their churning into right heart responses.

Not all the heart work will be done in the Break. The child will return for a debriefing to continue processing the offense, its ramifications, and better alternatives.

Remember that angry children don't like to be angry alone. They want to bait you into fighting with them. If they're successful, they shift the focus of the problem from their hearts to the interaction with their parents. Don't give them an excuse to focus on anything but their own heart problem.

Don't argue with an enraged child. Angry children aren't thinking clearly, and trying logic at these moments can add

fuel to the fire. Instead, let the Break do its job. Children eventually settle down. Sometimes it takes thirty seconds; other
times, twenty minutes or even an hour or more. Don't make
the mistake of setting a timer or prescribing how long a child
should sit in a Break. The goal isn't to punish a child—it's to
facilitate heart change.

You may need another consequence to get your child's
attention or to show you mean business, but then have your
child go back to the Break. It's not optional.

At first, you may only require that a child settle down in
the Break place and return to you ready to work on the problem. Most children lack the skills and understanding
necessary to go through all the repentance steps outlined in
chapter 14. They need parents to guide them through the
process. But, over time, children learn how to accomplish
more heart change on their own. As kids get older, some even
learn to put themselves in a Break and work through an
offense the way you've taught for years.

In some cases, unresponsive children take hours to settle
down and work on a problem. This is often frustrating for the
family that's trying to get out the door or keep up with busy
schedules. When a child is having a problem requiring discipline, you may choose to just make a comment about the
offense and then get out the door to stay on schedule. Other
times, however, you may decide the issue requires abandon-
ing the event or activity to deal with a heart problem. This is
especially helpful when the child is motivated to go to the
activity.

Greg's six-year-old daughter, Rachel, started one of her
temper tantrums just before the school bus was to arrive.
Greg decided working on the problem that day was more
important than riding the bus, so he waved the bus driver on
and told his daughter she wasn't free to go until they worked

on the problem. "That experience surprised my daughter. I don't think she expected me to stop her from going to school. It raised the level of importance of dealing with her anger and had a helpful impact. After we worked on the problem, I drove her to school and explained to her teacher why she was late." Another child might view missing the bus as a privilege, but Greg knew his daughter well enough to see the benefit of this approach with her.

When it isn't convenient to stop and use a Break, you're likely to get another opportunity sometime soon. Kids who have a problem in one area often show it elsewhere. The Break is only one approach to heart change but, used well and often, it can produce lasting results.

Why a Break Works

As we mentioned in a previous chapter, the paradigms children form in their hearts to guide their behavior and choices often contain incomplete or even false information. Children working from imperfect paradigms react in ineffective or harmful ways. Stopping a child's life temporarily helps him focus on a particular problem. A Break communicates that we're not going to live this way anymore.

IF YOUR CORRECTION ISN'T WORKING, MAYBE YOUR APPROACH IS COMPLICATING THE PROCESS.

Whether the offense is small or large, children are forced to reevaluate their paradigms. Correction helps a child embrace new ways of thinking, believing, and acting. The child that doesn't respond well to a word of correction often needs more self-reflection. The Break provides that opportunity. Although most children can't process the whole offense and determine a different course of action on their own, the Break helps them become more open to inner adjustments.

Children who resist correction often need more of it, unless, of course, parents need to change the way they do it. If your correction isn't working, maybe your approach is complicating the process. Be sure to evaluate both your child and yourself. The correction process is hard enough, especially when working with deep-rooted heart issues. Don't complicate the process with your own problems.

Starting Breaks in Your Family

If you're beginning the Break as a correction tool in your family, introduce it in a positive way. During a peaceful time, apart from conflict, meet with each of your children individually to explain the new plan. One mom shared with her seven-year-old about the Break this way: "You're getting older now, and it's time for us to make some adjustments in the way I correct you. I'm going to have you take a Break occasionally to help you change your heart. The location may change depending on where we are and what we're doing, but you'll sit in a particular place. While you're there, your job is to settle down and get ready to work on the problem. Then you can come back to me when you're ready, and I'll help you work through the rest of the process before you're free to go."

You might then, especially with younger children, practice taking a Break. "In a few minutes we're going to go to the park, but before we go, I want to practice this new Break idea. I'd like you to go over and sit on the floor by the table and then come back and tell me you're ready." This kind of practice in nonemotional moments can help children develop the Break routine. You may even identify small offenses during a particular day and use a Break with them first before you use it with bigger problems.

Sometimes during a discipline situation, children are reluctant to come out of the Break, and you'll need to coax them. Children who haven't experienced a heart-based approach to correction before may be resistant or uncertain. One mom told us, "My daughter went to the Break fine but then didn't want to come out. When I asked her why, she told me she didn't want to come back because she thought I'd just yell at her. I realized I had a tendency to lecture and yell and saw my approach was getting in the way of her heart change. My adjustments freed her to come out of the Break more easily, and to my surprise she was more willing to work on the problem. I was skeptical at first about the Break, but I now see the value of this approach."

When developing a new routine like the Break, you'll want to use it often to make it part of your interaction. Children may resist at first, but hang in there. The rewards are great. One mom sent us this e-mail describing her change from a Time-Out approach focusing on punishment to a Break technique that focused on the heart.

Dear Scott and Joanne,

I appreciated today's tip very much. It's an additional reinforcement for me. A few months back, one of your tips had a similar message: Take a Break vs. a Time Out.

My son is ten. I was then using the Time-Out method. It seemed like he'd determined to get over the ten-minutes thing, real fast, with a bad attitude. However, once I started using the Break method, my son seemed to respond differently. I felt we were beginning to connect on a deeper level regarding the problem at hand. Ron seemed to get an opportunity to think more about the offense and also to decide if there was a better way to deal with it while sitting at the bottom step of our stairway.

After a few months of consistency, my son is learning to manage some of his emotions better. Sometimes when he's about to say something that is unkind to me ... an old pattern ... he'll catch himself and say, "Mom, I stopped myself. I was going to say something that wasn't nice, but I changed my mind!"

My relationship with my son is becoming more purposeful and deeper. Thank you.

God Bless,
Leslie

Allowing God to Work

A complete heart change takes a lifetime, but the small day-to-day adjustments contribute to the long-term process. God often uses Breaks in our lives to work on our hearts. God gave Elijah a Break by the brook for several days when he felt discouraged and all alone, followed by a debriefing that strengthened Elijah's heart as he recognized God's plan. Paul was persecuting Christians, and God blinded him, giving him a Break to reevaluate his heart. The debriefing by Ananias after a few days helped him change his life goals. Moses, David, and Jacob each experienced heart change after periods of waiting and time alone.

A COMPLETE HEART CHANGE TAKES A LIFETIME, BUT THE SMALL DAY-TO-DAY ADJUSTMENTS CONTRIBUTE TO THE LONG-TERM PROCESS.

A Break is an adult skill. We all benefit from taking time to sit and think and let God work in our hearts. As we teach our children how to take a Break, we're developing a response pattern for them that they'll use as they get older. Yes, God uses other means to get our attention and change our hearts, but a Break is an excellent way to begin the repentance process.

Prayer

Lord, it seems my life is so busy that I would benefit from a Break every once in a while to consider my own heart. Please teach me to value my quiet time with you so I can adjust my heart to your will each day. I also pray that you give my children soft hearts and a willingness to respond well to correction. Use the Break in their lives to help them adjust their hearts in important ways. Give me the ability to be a helpful part of the correction process and not allow my own issues to cloud what needs to happen in my kids. Amen.

Chapter 16

Cross Your Heart

Richard doesn't take responsibility for his actions. He always blames someone or something else for the problems he gets himself into. His favorite targets are his brother and his mom, but it could be anyone—except himself. Richard is defensive, argumentative, and goes to great lengths to convince others that he's innocent or at least justified. Richard is forty-three years old, but his response is the same as many children today. In fact, many marriages and jobs could be saved if adults would learn how to take responsibility.

Taking responsibility for one's own actions is something children need to learn—and not just to make family life easier. It's a necessary part of success at any age. Many children, however, resist admitting they're wrong. Now's the time to teach it.

One of the benefits of taking responsibility is that it helps children who have developed a victim mentality. "Everybody picks on me. It's not my fault. There's nothing I can do about it." By teaching children to take responsibility, we empower them to be part of the solution instead of just part of the problem.

One way God moves us toward heart change is through confession. Even self-help groups such as Alcoholics Anonymous require confession before moving forward. During introductions in an AA meeting each person must say, "Hi, I'm Susie, and I am an alcoholic." Admitting you have a problem is necessary before you're able to find a solution. Confession, therefore, should be included regularly in the discipline process. Confession is a spiritual skill. It's simply acknowledging to God and often to others that you made a mistake or did the wrong thing. It's the first step toward meaningful change.

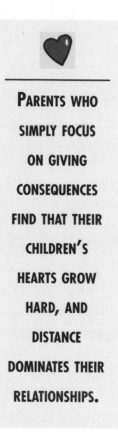

PARENTS WHO SIMPLY FOCUS ON GIVING CONSEQUENCES FIND THAT THEIR CHILDREN'S HEARTS GROW HARD, AND DISTANCE DOMINATES THEIR RELATIONSHIPS.

A Tool for Confession

Children often don't process offenses or correction well. They may be angry and determine in their hearts to get revenge using the silent treatment, yelling, or some other manipulative technique. Parents who simply focus on giving consequences find that their children's hearts grow hard, and distance dominates their relationships. The child may change outwardly but not on the inside, leaving parents frustrated, watching character weaknesses get worse.

Consequences may get a child's attention, but most kids need help processing the offense. We suggest that parents have a debriefing with children every time they have to redirect or discipline them. Children benefit from a discussion after even small offenses. We like to call this debriefing time a Positive Conclusion because it's designed to end every discipline time in a positive way.

When children come back from a Break or a consequence, they should know that the discipline time isn't over until the debriefing occurs. Knowing they'll always have a Positive Conclusion trains children to talk about problems, not just allow tension to linger in relationships. Sometimes this debriefing is a conversation about the problem and how it developed, but somewhere in the process the child should be required to answer the question, "What did *you* do wrong?"

It's interesting to watch how children respond to that question. Some answer by blaming—"She hit me." Others try to explain—"I didn't have any other choice." Still others rationalize or justify their response—"All the other kids were being mean too." These are simply attempts to dodge personal responsibility. Don't be deterred. Instead, say something like "We can talk about how others responded in a bit, but first I'd like you to answer the question, 'What did you do wrong?'"

Children may be reluctant to answer this question for many reasons, most of them heart-related. To confess mistakes to others, children must admit those mistakes to themselves—and that's where the heart work begins. Having a routine debriefing helps children practice confession and encourages them to make inner adjustments, not just external ones.

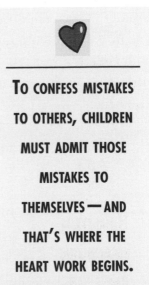

TO CONFESS MISTAKES TO OTHERS, CHILDREN MUST ADMIT THOSE MISTAKES TO THEMSELVES — AND THAT'S WHERE THE HEART WORK BEGINS.

Taking responsibility means doing the hard work of

readjusting what we believe, embracing different values, and acknowledging that change may be necessary—all requiring energy. The child who is lazy or looking for short-cuts will resist until life becomes unbearable or evidence stacks up significantly.

Some kids resort to lying and deception to cover up their offenses. Children who lie lack the courage to face the truth. Often the truth requires more work, humility, and confidence. Some children don't have the necessary character to take the high road of honesty, requiring parents to help them even more.

Confession Requires Humility

Some children perceive taking personal responsibility as weakness. They may even refuse, try to cover up their offense, or justify it in some way. Some kids use emotional intensity to keep their parents at bay and avoid taking responsibility. These children need to learn humility. That doesn't mean we humiliate our children. Yelling and making fun of kids breeds anger and defensiveness, not humility. Requiring children to confess is one step toward developing humility in their lives.

HUMILITY IS RECOGNIZING ONE'S NEED.

King Saul did the wrong thing. God told him not to bring any spoils back from the battle, but Saul did anyway. When confronted, Saul rationalized his disobedience by saying, "I brought these animals back to sacrifice to God" (1 Sam. 15:20–21). Saul's heart didn't follow after the Lord. David, on the other hand, sinned greatly with Bathsheba—but when confronted, he repented. He even wrote a psalm shortly after his sin became known and said,

"The sacrifices of God are a broken spirit; a broken and contrite heart" (51:17).

Humility is a heart issue and an essential ingredient in our lives. In fact, the greater the humility, the more a person can benefit from correction. The gift of God's grace empowers a person to change and is bigger than any sin we could commit. One of the prerequisites for receiving God's grace is humility. James 4:6 says, "God opposes the proud but gives grace to the humble." Your children need God's grace to change their hearts.

Humility is recognizing one's need. Too often our hearts deceive us into thinking we're self-sufficient, needing no one, and able to handle life without God or others. Children sometimes imagine they're invincible and don't need parental guidance. Disaster is usually right around the corner, and although children can't see it, their parents understand the danger.

God delights in humility because he knows a humble person will grow faster, learn more quickly, and make heart changes more readily. When Jesus was here on earth, he spent time with sinners because they were more ready for his message. When challenged, he said, "It is not the healthy who need a doctor, but the sick.... For I have not come to call the righteous, but sinners" (Matt. 9:12–13). Of course, we're all sinners, but some people are more willing to admit their need than others. Growth requires humility.

Of course children often have a hard time understanding this concept and view humility as weakness and a statement of their inadequacy. Your goal as a parent is to teach them humility without devastating them. They must learn that mistakes don't mean failure and admitting weakness is a sign of maturity. Most importantly, they need to learn that correction is a valuable gift.

Confession is just one way children learn humility. Look for ways to develop humility by helping children value others as more important than themselves. One dad told us, "Our son was in the invincible mode in his early teens. As a discipline, we gave him the assignment to take a mini-tape recorder around to several adults to ask a specific question and record the answer. He talked to about ten people and asked, 'What do you think I could do to make the most of my teenage years?' It was very interesting to hear people's responses, and it helped our son see that others had some good things to say." This kind of activity can help children develop humility and set the stage for a better response to correction.

An Apology—A Tool that Opens the Heart

Anthony was eleven years old when his mom brought him in for counseling because he had hit and pushed her. Mom responded well initially by making a big deal about it and communicating to Anthony that this was totally unacceptable. But after the fact, she refused to talk to him. Two days later, Anthony sat in my office. Even their ride to see me was silent. Mom didn't know how to end the discipline time.

When I met with Anthony alone, we talked about the situation. I asked him, "What did you do wrong?"

"I hit my mom."

"Anthony, why is that wrong?"

"You're not supposed to hit your parents."

"Yes, that's right, but also your actions say something about you that's important. You didn't respond well to authority. It's a bigger issue, you see. You may not like something that an authority does, but that doesn't mean you can be hurtful. What do you think you would do differently next time?"

"I don't know. Maybe I could talk about it."

"That's a good response, or maybe you'll need to get some help to know how to respond better. That's always an option too." Since Anthony was responding well to me, and I could tell that he felt remorse, I said, "I'll tell you what. I bet you know what you should do when you've done the wrong thing, right?"

"Yes. I should say I'm sorry."

"Saying you're sorry is good, but I'd like to teach you how to make a mature apology, Anthony. In fact, if you do this, you'll win your mom's heart. Would you like that?"

"Okay."

"I just asked you several questions and you gave me some good, honest answers. The answers to those three questions form the basis of a mature apology. Let me tell you what it would look like: 'Mom, I realize I was wrong when I hit you. I know that it's wrong because I wasn't responding well to authority, and you shouldn't hit your parents. Next time, I'll find a better way by talking about it. Will you please forgive me?' How does that sound, Anthony?"

"It sounds good."

"You see, when some kids say they're sorry, they do it with a sarcastic tone—'I'm so-o-o-rry!' What I'm teaching you is a mature way of apologizing. Many adults don't even know how to do this. Now, here's what we'll do. Let's practice it a few times, and then we'll bring your mom in here. I want you to lean forward, look into her eyes, apologize to her, and watch what happens. If you do this the way I'm telling you, you'll melt your mom's heart. After she responds to you, I'll send her back to the waiting room, and we'll talk some more."

After practicing four times to make sure Anthony had his apology down, I brought Mom in and asked her to sit facing her son. She didn't know what was going to happen. In fact, later she said she'd expected they were going to have to argue about the problem using me as a referee.

Anthony started his apology and did a fine job.

Mom began to cry. "I'm sorry too. Grabbing that CD out of your hand was the wrong way to treat you. Will you forgive me?" Then Mom hugged Anthony. After a few minutes, I asked Mom to step back out of the room while I continued to talk with her son.

"So, how did your mom respond?" I asked.

"She started crying."

"Yes, you touched her heart. Not only did she start to cry, but did you see what else she did? She hugged you. And she even apologized, too."

Anthony learned a valuable lesson that day I hope he'll never forget. He not only learned hitting Mom was wrong, but he also learned something about connecting on a heart level. That's the very special lesson we try to teach moms, dads, and kids every week. Conflict isn't just about what people do wrong. Conflict always provides an opportunity to understand a person's heart and deepen relationships. It often takes extra work, humility, and God's grace, but it's worth it in the end.

A Timely Apology

A well-planned apology from a parent can also be a window into a child's heart. Patrick recognized that he and his teenage daughter were at an impasse in their relationship. He now was realizing he hadn't tried to connect with her emotionally in earlier years, and they'd grown further and further apart. He'd focused on rules and behavior instead of the heart. He knew he had a problem.

He asked his daughter to help him move some boxes in the garage. She didn't want to help but begrudgingly agreed.

In the midst of the job, Dad stopped and said, "Tanya, I want to ask you to do something for me."

She looked at him with that "now what?" expression.

"I want to ask you to forgive me for not working on our relationship. I know I haven't done the best job at that, and I've lost you as a friend. I want to work on my relationship with you more. Will you forgive me?"

The apology took Tanya by surprise. They both began to cry. Patrick marks that day as the time he and his daughter began to connect on a heart level. An apology like that requires a tremendous amount of humility, more than some parents are willing to give. But ask yourself, "What would I do to win my child's heart?" Why not sacrifice by giving humility and gain so much in the process? Keep in mind the price for *not* connecting on a heart level is devastatingly high.

A Spiritual Issue

Confession is a spiritual exercise, and you can make it a regular part of your discipline times. Having a regular debriefing time after even small mistakes and offenses helps children develop a routine and makes the difficult times more palatable. Sometimes it may seem like children are saying what you want to hear just to get through the process. Don't give up. Hang in there and continue to help your children do right, all the time praying that God will do the deeper work in their hearts.

HAVING A REGULAR DEBRIEFING TIME AFTER EVEN SMALL MISTAKES AND OFFENSES HELPS CHILDREN DEVELOP A ROUTINE AND MAKES THE DIFFICULT TIMES MORE PALATABLE.

Remember that the habits of confession you establish now are good patterns. Pray that God will breathe life into the routines you use with your children. Even though the heart may not be in it now, the practice of confession is a good one and will make it easier for the child later on when the heart is ready.

Of course, the best way for children to understand humility is to see it in their parents. In one family counseling

THE BEST WAY FOR CHILDREN TO UNDERSTAND HUMILITY IS TO SEE IT IN THEIR PARENTS.

situation, the dad realized his abrupt approach with his wife and kids was causing several problems in family life. In one particularly touching session he said to his family, "I realize that I come on strong and raise my voice and overpower you when we disagree. Could you please tell me how that approach has hurt you?"

He then listened as, one by one, his three children and wife shared how his rough approach undermined his love for them. He didn't interrupt or try to defend himself. When they were done, he said, "I realize that my approach is wrong. It hurts people. I want to learn to be more kind and loving, especially when I disagree with you. I want to ask you to forgive me." We were in tears by then, and it was a special moment for all of us.

When Mom and Dad admit they're wrong and ask forgiveness, kids take note. When parents thank their children for things they do, it has a positive effect. Humility is a lifestyle, and the ability to confess is part of maturity. God knows confession is a window into the deepest parts of our heart—that's why he requires it from us in our relationship with him. When you teach your children how to confess, you're preparing them for their relationship with their heavenly Father. He longs for closeness, but sin separates us from fellowship with him. God has given us the tool of confession to open the door for forgiveness and greater closeness.

AS YOU WORK WITH YOUR CHILDREN ON THE DAY-TO-DAY ISSUES OF LIFE, YOU'RE PREPARING THEM TO KNOW, LOVE, AND SERVE GOD WITH ALL THEIR HEARTS.

As you work with your children on the day-to-day issues of life, you're preparing them to know, love, and serve God with all their hearts. Taking responsibility for one's actions isn't optional. It's part of God's curriculum for heart change.

Prayer

Lord, please give me the humility to admit my own weakness and to see that many of my strengths come from you and others who have helped me along life's path. Teach me how to help my children develop humility in their own lives so they can receive your grace and benefit from correction. Thank you for your patience with me. I look forward to the good things you will continue to do in my life. Amen.

Conclusion

Consider these two families:

Jack and Mary love each other, so they decided to just live together instead of getting married. It's been nine years now. They have three children, ages two, six, and eight. Parenting is a real struggle. Their kids don't cooperate much at home, and attempts at correction are usually fruitless. These parents do their job of giving consequences, but they don't see their kids changing significantly. Life goes on, but relationships seem distant. The kids fight and tattle. The bickering seems endless. Jack and Mary are frustrated, but it seems that this is the way kids are nowadays. They just don't listen and there's not much you can do about it. Everyone is busy. This family doesn't realize it, but they're headed for big trouble.

Kent and Elaine have been married for nine years. They've had conflict in their marriage and have had to work hard to learn new skills of relating. They also have three children. Their eight-year-old is facing challenges at school. He has trouble focusing and needs a lot of parental support to get assignments done and homework turned in. The kids tend to resist instructions, and correction is always a challenge. In the end, although it will require a lot of work, this family will be successful. They may not believe it at times, but they will win.

What's the difference between these two families? It has to do with the parents' hearts. Kent and Elaine have invited God to work in their hearts. That doesn't mean everything is easy. Their relationship together requires work, but their commitments and values force them deeper. As they both grow and change on a heart level, God is able to do some significant work. Their approach with their children focuses on the heart too. The kids experience challenges and have selfish tendencies, but Dad and Mom approach those problems with deeper values in mind. They're continually looking for ways to allow God to work through them in their kids' lives.

Jack and Mary don't have a clue. We don't say this to be unkind—it's just that their understanding of what a family ought to be is so molded by our culture that they're missing the most important things in life. Their hearts are filled with desires and values that miss what God offers to them. It saddens us as we try to help families like this, because they seem not to get it. They're disappointed in what they see in their children but are unwilling to make the commitment necessary to see real change. They resist looking at their own hearts and want to blame the problems on their kids.

Fortunately, these two families are neighbors. Recently Jack and Mary attended Kent and Elaine's church. While there, they saw a love they hadn't experienced before. Last month, Jack and Mary committed themselves to Christ. They want something more in life. They now see the need to make changes in their own hearts. Their whole perspective on family life is changing too. They're planning a wedding this summer because they want to do things right. They're determined to follow God's plan for their family, and now they realize that it starts with the heart.

Sometimes Jack and Mary ask, "Is it too late? Have we messed up our kids so much that they can't get straightened out?" We assure them it's never too late with God. He delights in helping individuals and families at any age or stage. God changes people, and he starts in the heart.

Inviting God into their lives doesn't mean this family will

live problem-free, but they now have a framework to live by and God guiding them along the path. It means that their choices about family life are different now, and the way they discipline takes on a new perspective. Jack and Mary are on the right track, and they, too, will be successful as they face life's challenges.

In this book, we've shared three ways you can touch your child's heart. Emotional connectedness, instruction, and correction are the tools you need to go deeper. As you hone your approach, train your children in new ways, and pray diligently for God's grace, you'll see changes you never thought possible.

But this is only the beginning of the positive influence you can have on your children. The heart is a rich place where convictions are held, forgiveness replaces anger, and the conscience becomes a tool for sensitivity in relationships both with God and with others. Once you develop these first three tools in your family, then bigger and better heart changes are on their way.

READERS' GUIDE

*For Personal Reflection or
Group Discussion*

READERS' GUIDE

"I love teaching Sunday school. Sometimes I just wish I could get these truths from the kids' heads to their hearts."

That statement is true not only for Sunday school teachers, but also for parents who want to see lasting change in their kids. That's easier said than done, however. Parents often wish they could go deeper but just can't seem to find the right words, the best time, or an effective method.

A heart-based approach to parenting requires a special way of thinking. In fact, as we move in the right directions with our children, we see heart changes that God wants *us* to make as well. This readers' guide is designed to get you thinking and pondering a little more about the principles taught in this book. The questions are designed with heart-change in mind because, as parents, we all need a tune-up as well.

You can use these discussion questions on your own for further contemplation, or you may want to meet with others for group discussion. Either way, it's our prayer that you'll be able to integrate the concepts from this book into your parenting. We pray you'll be able to transfer them from your head to your heart.

INTRODUCTION: SEE WITH NEW EYES

1. Jesus rebuked the Pharisees in Matthew 12:33–35. What principle was Jesus trying to teach?

2. Behavior modification uses rewards and punishment to change behavior. When might this be helpful and when is it dangerous?

3. Two brothers fight constantly, using meanness, sarcasm, and hurtful words as ammunition for their battles. If you

approached this problem from a heart perspective, what might you do differently from the parent who uses only behavior modification?

4. What do you see in your own heart that might be hindering your parenting?

CHAPTER 1: WHAT IS THE HEART? (PART 1)

1. Look back over the five functions of the heart mentioned in this chapter. Which one stands out as something you'd like to see strengthened in your child's heart? Why?

2. Disappointment happens when you set your heart on something and then don't get it. What tips might you give a child about ways to handle disappointment?

3. Give an example of a way you and your child connect on a heart level.

4. In Matthew 9:4, Jesus was able to see into the hearts of the teachers of the law and he challenged them. Imagine being in their place. What issues were they wrestling with?

CHAPTER 2: WHAT IS THE HEART? (PART 2)

1. Go back through the various sections of this chapter and pick one heart function you'd like to see developed in your child. Why does that one stick out for you?

2. What might parents do to strengthen a child's conscience?

3. Name three convictions you have in your heart that you wish you could transfer to your child. What are some ways to help children develop convictions?

4. How can you help children connect with God even if they haven't yet given their hearts to him?

CHAPTER 3: WILL I OR WON'T I?

1. Two children are playing. One is strong willed and the other seems content to follow. How do you know when to step in to set limits on the dominant child or encourage the unmotivated child to take initiative?

2. Would you consider yourself more or less strong willed than your child? How does this affect your interaction?

3. How might you help a child who seems insensitive to social cues and bulldozes over others?

4. What are the advantages and disadvantages of being strong willed or unmotivated?

CHAPTER 4: DO IT LIKE YOU MEAN IT

1. What kind of things do your children like to talk about? How can you turn those conversations into learning experiences?

2. What prevents you from listening to your children?

3. Jesus said, "Where your treasure is, there will your heart be also" (Matt. 6:2). What's something you wish your family would treasure more? What are some first steps you could take to make that happen?

4. How might you advise a dad who feels like his daughter doesn't talk to him? What practical things might he do to increase communication?

CHAPTER 5: EMOTIONS HAVE FEELINGS TOO

1. Read Galatians 5:22–23. The first three fruits of the Spirit are commonly considered emotions. How will a person's feelings be different when the Holy Spirit is allowed to work?

2. Describe a time when your first cues about a problem or situation were emotional ones (e.g., you could feel the situation before you actually understood it).

3. Describe a situation when you or your child connected by one of you touching the other emotionally.

4. What's a common emotion your child experiences and how might you use it as an opportunity to grow closer?

CHAPTER 6: TURN ON THEIR HEART LIGHTS

1. In John 13:33, Jesus told his disciples he was going away. They were concerned. How did Jesus connect with them emotionally in John 14:1–4?

2. What are some ways you like to be loved? How does your child like to experience love? Are you similar to or different from your child in this area, and how do you handle the differences?

3. Describe a way your family tends to connect emotionally. What makes the connection happen?

4. Most parents are extremely busy. What suggestions might you give to help on-the-go parents connect emotionally with their children?

CHAPTER 7: AVOIDING CONGESTIVE HEART FAILURE

1. God talks about emotional health in terms of "peace guarding your heart" in Philippians 4:7. What advice does God give in verses 7 and 8 for maintaining that peace?

2. When you get upset, what are some things you do to help yourself recover and return to a balanced state?

3. What can you do to remain calm when your child is upset? How can you discuss emotional challenges with your child without losing your composure?

4. Choose one idea from this chapter you'd like to explore to improve the emotional climate in your home. What might be a first step?

CHAPTER 8: MAKING THE CONNECTION

1. Describe an experience in your life in which living without something helped you become more grateful for it (food, finances, health, and so forth).

2. What times in a given day or week are best for your family to exchange facts and information about their lives?

3. Name several gifts of love you can give your children that don't cost money.

4. Parenting is sometimes disappointing because children are resistant. What can you do to prevent your own heart

from accumulating anger when your children resist or reject your leadership?

CHAPTER 9: TALKING TO YOURSELF

1. What situations tend to evoke anger in your child? What misconceptions might he or she be repeating in his or her heart that fuel that anger?

2. When parents identify thinking errors in their children, what are some ways they react that hinder reflection and change?

3. What are some good things your children already say in their hearts that you want to encourage? (These things may help them demonstrate courage, persistence, or patience.)

4. When you get upset about something and are trying to remain composed, what kinds of things do you say in your heart?

CHAPTER 10: TEACHING YOUR CHILD'S HEART

1. Describe one thing you learned from your father and one thing you learned from your mother. (Keep in mind that sometimes we learn what *not* to do—but first, try to pick something you appreciate about both parents.)

2. Name something you wish your child would learn. What creative ways might you use to teach it?

3. What are some ways parents teach their children to develop the mind? What does it mean to teach children in a way that focuses on the heart?

4. In Matthew 12:33–34, Jesus used the illustration of a tree to rebuke the Pharisees regarding their hearts. What message was he was trying to communicate to them?

CHAPTER 11: MEDITATION MANAGEMENT

1. Read Proverbs 20:5. What does this verse say about the heart and about your role in helping your children change?

2. What's something you tend to meditate on? How do you know when mulling over this issue, situation, or experience is helpful and when your thinking has crossed the line and become counterproductive?

3. What problems might you see in your children that come from wrong thinking or meditating on the wrong things? What do you wish they would meditate on instead?

4. What Bible verses are helpful for you to meditate on and keep you on (or bring you back to) the right track in your heart?

5. Which of the four areas of change mentioned in this chapter might be helpful to work on in your family?

CHAPTER 12: A LIGHT ON THE PATH TO HEART CHANGE

1. What are some of the roadblocks that prevent parents from teaching the Bible to their children?

2. Think back to a recent sermon you heard. What was the Bible message and how did it feed your heart?

3. Think of a problem your child has right now. What quality would address that problem and what Bible verse would teach that truth?

4. When might be a good time for you to talk about the Bible with your children? What barriers will you have to overcome to get that regular dialogue flowing?

Chapter 13: Constructive Correction

1. What observations about correction might you make from these verses: Proverbs 15:5, 15:23, and 10:23.

2. Take an honest look into your own heart for a moment. Why do you sometimes resist correction instead of embracing it?

3. Mark, age fourteen, won't listen to correction. He endures it as a necessary evil, and trying to reach his heart feels like trying to cut into cement. What suggestions might you give to help Mark's parents correct him in meaningful ways?

4. What is one attitude or behavior that needs correction in your child? What approach to that one thing might be most productive?

Chapter 14: Turn Around for a Change

1. Describe a time when you saw true repentance in your child. What did it look like?

2. When your child is confronted, what's the typical response? What roadblocks get in the way of true repentance?

3. The first part of repentance is settling down and becoming willing to talk about the problem. What can you do to facilitate this step in your child?

4. Why do children blame problems on others and refuse to take personal responsibility? Why is admitting you're wrong so important for a change of heart?

CHAPTER 15: DEFIBRILLATING YOUR CHILD'S HEART

1. When your heart starts to churn about something, such as an upcoming appointment or being treated unfairly, what's the primary emotion you feel? How does your churning tend to end?

2. Consider a problem your child experiences, such as arguing, meanness, anger, or disrespect. How might you take action earlier to stop the escalation?

3. In Acts 9:8–9, God used a Break to help change Saul's heart. What do you imagine Saul might have said in his heart during that three-day period that helped him redirect his life?

4. Consider one of the more difficult problems your child experiences. What kind of heart adjustments would help, and how might you use a Break to motivate your child to consider a different direction?

CHAPTER 16: CROSS YOUR HEART

1. Philippians 2:8 says Jesus Christ humbled himself and became obedient. What do humility and obedience have in common?

2. How can you help your children develop humility without humiliating them?

3. Recall a time when you apologized to your kids in a way that touched their hearts. Why is a parent's apology so powerful?

4. Why do children blame problems on others, and why is that so dangerous?

Parenting
is
Heart
WORK
Video Series

If you liked the book, you'll love the movies! Use this eight-part video series in your church, small group, or even in your own family. Learn how to apply the concepts you've read in this book to the common routines in family life.

In this video series you'll learn:

- A 5-step process for giving instructions that will build cooperation and responsibility in your kids.
- Seven categories of consequences to fill up your "Toolbox."
- How to address thinking errors in children.
- A plan for correction to help kids make lasting changes.
- Plus many more practical ideas to use every day.

The videos were filmed before a live audience of parents and children. Using drama, Bible stories, and lots of illustrations, Dr. Turansky and Mrs. Miller will energize you and provide you with tools you need to strengthen your family. Use the reproducible Leader's Guide to give handouts to all participants. Children learn truths that complement what the parents are learning as they enjoy the activity-based eight-session Treasure Hunters curriculum.

NATIONAL CENTER *for* BIBLICAL PARENTING | 76 Hopatcong Drive, Lawrenceville, NJ 08648-4136
Phone: (800) 771-8334
Email: parent@biblicalparenting.org
Web: www.biblicalparenting.org

Your family is just a few steps away from a miracle—and that miracle starts with you!

Parenting *is* Heart WORK

Audio Series and Workbooks

Listen to nationally known teachers Dr. Turansky and Mrs. Miller as they unpack strategic routines of family life. Learn how to give day-to-day instructions in a way that builds cooperation and responsibility. Hear practical ideas for connecting with your kids emotionally so that their hearts will be soft and teachable. Each session comes with a 20-page workbook that walks you through the content step-by-step, showing you how to put the truths into practice with your children.

These workbooks and CDs are designed to help you integrate the material into your family. Answer the questions in the workbook, look up the scriptures, reflect on the teaching, and watch yourself make significant changes in the ways you relate. When parents change, children change. You'll love the difference.

NATIONAL CENTER for BIBLICAL PARENTING

76 Hopatcong Drive, Lawrenceville, NJ 08648-4136
Phone: (800) 771-8334
Email: parent@biblicalparenting.org
Web: www.biblicalparenting.org

HOME
Improvement

Eight Tools for Effective Parenting

Dr. Scott Turansky and
Joanne Miller, RN, BSN

Learn eight principles every family needs. This is the parenting book you can read to your kids. The beginning of every chapter follows a fictional family through typical challenges. Craig and Marlene struggle with their two children but then discover parenting tools to help with the common problems we all face. The second part of each chapter teaches you how to implement that tool in your family. Children catch a vision for change as you read the narrative story with them. They get a glimpse of how the changes you're trying to make will help the whole family be successful.

Purchase this book now at your local Christian bookstore.

ISBN 0-78144-151-X
192 pages

In This Book You Will Learn...

- *Four truths that motivate you to continue on when you're tired, discouraged, and ready to give up.*
- *A unique concept that reveals the cues that tell your children when they must obey.*
- *A six-step "Secret Weapon" you can use when all else seems to have failed and you need a bigger plan to help children develop character, not just change their behavior.*
- *Three practical ways to be a coach to your kids and help them learn from life.*
- *One small but powerful ingredient to add to your parenting to help your children develop wisdom.*
- *A three-step plan to help your children deal with anger through frustration management, anger control, rage reduction, and releasing bitterness.*

Free *Email* Parenting Tips

Receive guidance and inspiration a couple of times a week in your inbox. Free parenting tips give practical suggestions to help you relate better to your kids and help your kids change their hearts, not just their behavior.

The National Center for Biblical Parenting is here to help you. Co-founders, Dr. Scott Turansky and Joanne Miller, RN, BSN are committed to encouraging and equipping parents.

Visit www.biblicalparenting.org and sign up today for free email parenting tips.

If you're interested in a high-energy, spiritually-energizing live seminar with Dr. Scott Turansky and Joanne Miller, RN, BSN, please contact the National Center for Biblical Parenting.

Did you find this book helpful? Please send us an email and let us know how this study has helped you and your family. Reach us at parent@biblicalparenting.org.

NATIONAL CENTER *for* **BIBLICAL PARENTING** | 76 Hopatcong Drive, Lawrenceville, NJ 08648-4136
Phone: (800) 771-8334
Email: parent@biblicalparenting.org
Web: www.biblicalparenting.org